CONTENTS

KINGSTON LACY

Dorset

THE NATIONAL TRUST

Kingston Lacy is on the B3082 Blandford–Wimborne road,
1½ miles west of Wimborne.

Acknowledgements

The late Daphne Bankes transcribed letters and documents in
the Library and Muniment Room at Kingston Lacy in the
1930s which have been invaluable. Hugh Jacques and Sarah
Bridges at the Dorchester Record Office, where the latter is
cataloguing the Bankes archives, have been of the greatest
help. Research has been undertaken there by William Riviere,
Anthony Kilroy, George Clarke and John Cornforth.
Antony Cleminson unravelled the architectural history of the
house and drew the floor plans. For this new guide Chapter
Three and the opening of Chapter Nine have been written by
George Clarke; Chapter Ten by Elizabeth Barthold, the
American Icomos scholar. Alastair Laing has written Chapter
Seven and revised the picture and sculpture entries compiled
by St John Gore, who did much of the preliminary work on
the collection. Anthony du Boulay has contributed the
ceramics entries, T. G. H. James the section on the Egyptian
collection. We would also like to thank the following:
Dr Andrew Ciechanowiecki, Dr Mary Crawford Volk,
Sir Brinsley Ford, Dr Kenneth Garlick, Mrs Enriqueta Harris,
Prof. Michael Jaffé, Norman Lewis, Sir Oliver Millar,
Dr Jennifer Montagu, Anthony Mould, Dr Mauro Natale,
Martin Papworth, Dr Hella Robels, Dr Malcolm Rogers,
Pierre Rosenberg, John Somerville, Julien Stock, Dr John
Walsh, Dr Philip Ward-Jackson, Prof. Humphrey Whitfield.

Anthony Mitchell

Photographs: Country Life Picture Library p. 12; Courtauld Institute
of Art p. 15; Fotomas Index p. 13; National Trust pp. 10, 18, 21, 27,
28, 34 (above), 36, 83, 84; National Trust Photographic Library pp. 29,
34 (below), 35, 67; NTPL/Roy Fox pp. 40, 41; NTPL/Angelo Hornak
p. 32; NTPL/Christopher Hurst pp. 11, 19 (above), 48; NTPL/James
Mortimer pp. 1, 4, 30, 31, 43, 45, 49, 52, 53, 65, 71, 73, 80;
NTPL/Alasdair Ogilvie pp. 87, 92; NTPL/Richard Pink pp. 6, 8, 9,
89, 90, 91, back cover; NTPL/Rupert Truman front cover, p. 85;
NTPL/Derrick E. Witty pp. 7, 16, 17, 19 (below), 22, 25, 26, 33, 38,
39, 50, 55, 56, 60, 69, 76, 81.

First published in Great Britain in 1994 by the National Trust

©1994 The National Trust
Registered charity no. 205846
Reprinted 1997, 2000, 2002, 2003, 2004, 2005, 2006; revised 1998

ISBN 1-84359-042-5
ISBN 978-1-84359-042-2

Designed by James Shurmer

Phototypeset in Monotype Bembo Series 270
by Intraspan Ltd, Smallfield, Surrey (SG1421)

Printed by Hawthornes for National Trust (Enterprises) Ltd,
Heelis, Kemble Drive, Swindon, Wilts SN2 2NA

INTRODUCTION

'Where will there be in any private house in England a family monument of equal magnificence?' wrote William John Bankes from Venice in 1855 shortly before he died. He was referring to the culmination of his patronage of Carlo Marochetti – three life-size bronze figures of Sir John Bankes, Lord Chief Justice of the Common Pleas, Lady Bankes clasping the key of Corfe Castle, and their monarch, King Charles I, in the Loggia at the first flight of his marble staircase. It was the last, crowning element of his re-creation over twenty years of the Bankes family seat, yet he did not live to see it.

Sir John Bankes sprang from a modest yeoman family in Cumberland to become an able lawyer and a moderate man who played a key part in the confrontation between King and Parliament that resulted in the Civil War. He purchased the old royal estates of Corfe Castle in 1635 and Kingston Lacy in 1632–6, dying at the exiled Court in Oxford in 1644. 'Brave Dame Mary' withstood two long sieges of Corfe for the King, but the castle was finally taken by treachery in 1646 and ruined. It remains a romantic symbol of the Royalist cause.

Their son Ralph, knighted at the Restoration as reward for the Bankeses' loyalty, built a new family seat in 1663 twenty miles away at Kingston Lacy. Kingston Hall was designed by Sir Roger Pratt and still contains much of Sir Ralph's collection of pictures, one of the earliest surviving made by a member of the gentry.

The first transformation of the house was made by Henry Bankes the Younger in the 1780s with his architect Robert Furze Brettingham, whom he met in Rome. Their surviving rooms are the Library and the Saloon, with its chimneypiece by Flaxman and coved ceiling painted by Cornelius Dixon. Henry enlarged the park to its present shape, extensively planting trees and doing away with the old formal garden.

In 1829 Henry wrote, 'the bricks are deposited opposite my window for the foundation of William's Obelisk ... I submit to it as a disorder in the Bankes family, which sometimes passes over one generation, like madness or gout, or the king's evil, and breaks out again in the next: my uncle ... could not help erecting two Obelisks.' The elegant pink granite obelisk from Philae was the major trophy of his son William's pioneering travels in Egypt and Syria. His Egyptian antiquities, now arranged in the Billiards Room, form the sole surviving gentleman's collection from the early days of British Egyptology. William acquired paintings in Spain in 1812–15, travelled widely in Syria, penetrating to Palmyra and Petra, and made two expeditions up the Nile beyond Abu Simbel. On his way home in 1820 he bought important pictures in Bologna and visited his Cambridge friend Byron in Venice and Ravenna. Between 1835 and 1841 William and Charles Barry transformed Kingston Hall into the house we know today, encased in Chilmark stone, with a new cupola and balustrade and a Roman staircase of Carrara marble. In 1841 he was charged with a homosexual offence and went to live abroad, where he devoted the rest of his life to designing and commissioning the fittings in marble and carved wood for Kingston Lacy, as it now came to be called. The house is his monument and the Spanish Room his golden masterpiece.

Kingston Lacy contains more than a great family collection of paintings, for the rooms retain the relatively undisturbed atmosphere of its heyday in Edwardian times. The Drawing Room and the White Bedroom especially express the taste and strong personality of Henrietta Bankes, whose son Ralph bequeathed the house and estate to the National Trust in 1981.

(Left) The Saloon

CHAPTER ONE

SIR JOHN BANKES AND BRAVE DAME MARY

Kingston Lacy was probably established during the Anglo-Saxon period as the administrative centre of a large royal estate within the manor of Wimborne. (The first direct reference to Kingston is in 1170, when it is called 'Kingestune', in its earliest form probably *cyning tun*, which means 'the king's manor or estate'. 'Lacy' was taken from one of the medieval tenants, the de Lacys, Earls of Lincoln.) The Domesday Book of 1086 records that the royal manor of Wimborne had land for 45 plough teams and eight water-mills. It has been estimated that the estate at this time covered over 20,000 acres, so it must have been a substantial enterprise. During the medieval period the Crown sometimes managed the manor directly, but more often granted it to supporters: in the twelfth century the Earls of Leicester; in the thirteenth and fourteenth centuries the de Lacys. From the fourteenth to the sixteenth centuries Kingston Lacy was part of the royal Duchy of Lancaster.

The site of the medieval manor house was revealed in 1990 when storms uncovered medieval building debris in the roots of fallen trees in the park, within Court Close, 150 yards north of the present house and east of Snake Pond. The footings of walls can be seen as earthworks here, and fragments of glazed ridge tiles and fourteenth- to fifteenth-century pottery were also found. The accounts of the Duchy of Lancaster record the fourteenth- and fifteenth-century repairs to the various buildings within the manor. The outer bailey contained the working buildings such as the stables, the granary and the wool shed. The wall of the inner ward enclosed the domestic buildings, such as the manor house, chapel and bakehouse. In addition to the buildings, farmland and woodland, there was also a large area of hunting land which included two deer-parks at Holt and Kingston Lacy, each with its own hunting lodge. Serving the Kingston Lacy deer-park was Lodge Farm, which survives as a stone-built first-floor hall-house of the late fourteenth century, indicating the grandeur of medieval Kingston Lacy (see Chapter Ten).

The Kingston estate was important enough to warrant no fewer than five royal visits during the reign of Edward I. The lord of Kingston in the late fourteenth century was Edward III's son John of Gaunt, Duke of Lancaster, who also visited the manor on several occasions. In 1381 preparations were made to accommodate the administrative council of the Duchy of Lancaster:

... And on cleaning the great stable against the coming of the lord's council in September this year 4d. And on straw purchased for bedding both in the chambers and

(Left) Lodge Farm, which served the deer-park on the medieval Kingston estate

(Right) Chief Justice Sir John Bankes (1589–1644); by Gilbert Jackson, 1643 (No.9; Library)

in the stable for the same time 6d. Purchase of goblets, dishes and platters for those coming to the council. And on three dozen ridge pieces purchased for the roof of the house 3s.

Few of those who held the manor lived there, an exception being John of Gaunt's grandson, John Beaufort, 1st Duke of Somerset, who died in 1444 and whose tomb is in Wimborne Minster. His daughter Lady Margaret Beaufort, Countess of Richmond and mother of Henry VII, was brought up at Kingston Lacy and regained the estate after the victory of her son at the Battle of Bosworth in 1485. By this time the manor house had fallen into ruins, and in 1495 it was being used as a quarry for Wimborne Minster, Margaret Beaufort having made Canford the administrative centre of the estate. According to the antiquary John Leland, writing in the early sixteenth century, 'Ther hath beene sins a fair maner place caullid Kingston-Haul, and this is now in a manner clerely defacid.'

We know little about life at Kingston Lacy in the sixteenth century, although it appears that much of the open hunting land was enclosed during this period. In 1603 James I gave the manor to Sir Charles Blount, 1st Earl of Devonshire, whose brilliant military career culminated with the pacification of Ireland. His son, Mountjoy Blount, 1st Earl of Newport, who succeeded him in 1606, sold Holt Chase, Badbury Warren and the manor and refectory of Canford Prior in 1632, and the rest of the ancient manor of Kingston Lacy in 1636 to Sir John Bankes for £11,400 'of lawful English money'.

The Bankeses were an old Cumberland yeoman family living in the vale of Keswick. After attending the local grammar school, John Bankes had gone up to Queen's College, Oxford in 1604 at the age of fifteen, leaving without a degree to enter Gray's Inn in London as a law student in 1607. According to Fuller's *Worthies*, 'Sir John Bankes was born at Keswick, of honest parents, who perceiving him judicious and industrious, bestowed good breeding on him in Gray's Inn, in hope he should attain to preferment; wherein they were not deceived.' He was called to the Bar in 1614 and in the 1620s became MP for Wootton Bassett and then for Morpeth. In March 1622 he purchased a half-share in the black lead or graphite mines in Borrowdale,

'Brave Dame Mary' (1598–1661); enamel miniature by Henry Bone (Drawing Room)

which became a useful, if intermittent, source of income for the family (see Chapter Three). Bankes rose rapidly on the national stage. In 1630 the King made him Attorney-General to the infant Prince Charles, and in 1634 his own Attorney-General and a knight; it was said at the time 'that he exceeds Bacon in eloquence, Chancellor Ellesmere in judgement, and William Noy in law'.

Sir John's legal reputation had by 1635 brought him a sufficient fortune to acquire the ancient royal castle of Corfe on the Isle of Purbeck. A year later he completed the purchase of the Kingston Lacy estate. 'Henceforward he was in close personal touch with Charles I, who, though critical of Sir John's independent judgement which amounted to stubbornness, never lost his affection for his Attorney-General,' wrote Viola Bankes in *A Dorset Heritage*. In 1637, in spite of some private Puritan sympathies, he was obliged to carry out the arbitrary prosecution of the Puritan pamphleteer William Prynne in the Star Chamber. In the same year he represented the Crown in the Ship Money case, speaking for three days against John Hampden, who had challenged the legality of this hated tax. In 1641 he was promoted to Chief Justice of the Common Pleas.

He remained at his post in Westminster after the King left London for the north at the outbreak of the Civil War in 1642, but soon obeyed the royal summons to join the Privy Council in York. However, he offended the King by not opposing the Militia Bill and wrote in an anguished letter to Mr Green, the member for Corfe:

... I have given him my opinion on it. I have told him it is not safe for me to deliver anie opinion in things which are voted in the housses. You know how cautious I have been in this particular; I have studied all meanes which way matters may be brought to a good conclusion between the king and the housses, all high wayes of force will be distructive; and if we should have civill warrs, it would make us a miserable people, and might introduce foreign powers; therefore, there is no other way left but the way of accomodation ...

So he was never offered the great seal when the position of Lord Chancellor became vacant. By his caution and moderation, however, and because of the solid respect in which he was held by his moderate friends in Westminster, he came to assume the role of mediator between King and Parliament at this momentous time. This only changed in the summer of 1643, when at the Salisbury assizes he led the judges in their indict-

ment for high treason of those Parliamentary leaders who continued in arms against the King.

After the Battle of Edgehill in October 1642, Sir John accompanied the Court to Oxford, where he liberally assisted the royal finances: Charles I's receipt for the substantial sum of £525 for twenty horses is displayed in the Drawing Room at Kingston Lacy. The Civil War not only depleted Sir John's fortune, but also devastated the home he had created at Corfe Castle, with its family portraits by Van Dyck and lavish furnishings, which included tapestries and gilt leather hangings. In the words of John Hutchins, the historian of Dorset:

His integrity was acknowledged by his very enemies, and the ruined walls of his seat at Corfe Castle remain a monument of his loyalty ... he garrisoned Corfe Castle and left his lady to defend it, which she bravely did, with the assistance of the neighbouring gentry, maintaining two sieges, and at last lost it only by treachery.

In 1618 he had married Mary Hawtrey, daughter of Mary Altham and Ralph Hawtrey, whose family was long established at Ruislip near London. She bore him six sons and eight daughters, some of whom were with her at Corfe. In 1643 'Brave Dame Mary' staunchly defended the castle during the first siege by Parliamentary forces, while Sir John was on circuit duty in Salisbury. They enjoyed a brief period of domestic tranquillity together in the family home later that year before he returned to serve his king in Oxford. There Sir John died, aged 55, on 28 December 1644, tended by his two elder daughters, Lady Borlase and Lady Jenkinson, in whose house he was living.

The second siege of Corfe lasted 48 days and was only ended, in February 1646, by the treachery of a member of the garrison who admitted Parliamentary troops to the castle disguised as reinforcements. Lady Bankes was forced to agree a truce and Colonel Bingham, an honourable Dorset man, permitted her to leave with the keys of the castle as a mark of her courage. They still hang over the chimneypiece in the Library at Kingston Lacy. Brave Dame Mary survived her husband by another seventeen years, living latterly at Damory Court, Blandford, as Corfe Castle had been reduced to ruins by Parliamentary gunpowder.

The siege of Corfe Castle: Carlo Marochetti's bronze relief in the Loggia

CHAPTER TWO
SIR RALPH BANKES AND KINGSTON HALL

Despite the upheavals of the Civil War, Lady Bankes's sons received a first-class education. Her eldest, John (1626–56), went up to Oriel College in Royalist Oxford in July 1643 and was painted while still a student with his tutor, Sir Maurice Williams, probably by Francis Cleyn (No. 133). We next hear of him travelling from France to Italy at the end of 1646 and signing the visitors' book at the University of Padua in June 1647. Inscriptions in his books still in the Kingston Lacy Library give us further clues about his movements: 'Paris 1647', 'Geneva August 1647'. Lady Bankes's second son, Ralph (?1631–77), probably accompanied John on his European tour, as he inscribed his name in a book in the same way at Rouen in 1648. Her youngest, Jerome (1635/6–86), also studied at Oxford and toured the Continent, dining with his cousin Edward Altham at the Jesuit English College in Rome in July 1654. Altham went

so far as to become a Catholic, to Lady Bankes's horror, and painted himself as a hermit – No. 70. Jerome reached as far south as Naples, where he was painted by Stanzione (No. 3).

Although abroad for much of the 1640s and 1650s, the Bankes brothers did not neglect their interests at home. In 1647 Lady Bankes and her children paid large sums of money to regain the family property confiscated by Parliament after the second siege of Corfe; Cromwell also restored the land that had been settled on her by her husband. They seem then to have been left in peace during the Commonwealth. John Bankes enjoyed his restored inheritance only briefly, as he died unmarried at the age of 30 in 1656.

John was succeeded by his brother Ralph, the builder of the first great house at Kingston Lacy. Pale-skinned and with fair hair, worn long in the

Pratt's elevation for the north front of Kingston Hall

Sir Ralph Bankes (?1631–77), the builder of Kingston Hall; by Sir Peter Lely (No. 7; Library)

fashion of the day, he followed his father into the law, also training at Gray's Inn. By the late 1650s he had restored the family fortunes and begun to indulge the artistic tastes probably acquired during his travels on the Continent. In 1659 he was living in comfortable circumstances in Gray's Inn and was part of a cultured circle that included the most fashionable painter of the age, Peter Lely, and the gentleman-architect Roger Pratt, who was living not far away in the Inner Temple (see Chapter Seven).

Ralph Bankes sat in Richard Cromwell's Parliament in 1659 for the family seat of Corfe Castle and remained an MP until his death in 1677, being active mainly in safeguarding his Dorset interests. With the Restoration of Charles II in 1660, he was knighted at Canterbury and made a gentleman of the privy chamber in recognition of the price his family had paid for their loyalty to the Crown. The following year he married Mary Brune of Athelhampton, from an old Dorset family. Although the daughter of a Parliamentary colonel, she later became a Roman Catholic; more importantly from Sir Ralph's point of view, she was an heiress worth £1,200 a year. Two years later in 1663 they set about building a new family seat, Kingston Hall, employing Roger Pratt as their architect.

Sir Ralph may have first met Pratt abroad in the 1640s, as the latter spent much of that decade in France and Italy studying Classical Roman architecture and the buildings and writings of Palladio, Fréart and Scamozzi inspired by it. In 1649 Pratt returned to England, where he found the state of architecture woefully backward by comparison. The only modern English buildings he respected were the Queen's House in Greenwich, the Banqueting House in Whitehall and the classical portico of old St Paul's, all designed by Inigo Jones. It is not surprising, therefore, that Kingston Hall should have been attributed to Jones until Pratt's notes were published in 1928 and its real architect was rediscovered.

Pratt's first house, Coleshill in Berkshire, was his masterpiece. It was built for his cousin during the 1650s and became the model not only for his four other commissions, but also for the Restoration country house. His surviving drawing for the north elevation of Kingston Hall shows the exterior to have been very similar to Coleshill – of two main storeys, nine bays wide, with stone quoins and mullion casement windows (much later replaced, as at Coleshill, with sashes). The principal floor, or *piano nobile*, was raised above a half-basement and entered directly at the centre up a flight of stairs, as

Coleshill in Berkshire, Roger Pratt's masterpiece, which was destroyed by fire in 1952

Clarendon House, Piccadilly, built by Pratt in 1664–7
for the Lord Chancellor, Edward Hyde; engraving after
J. Spilbergh

Pratt recommended: 'An ascent on the outside of a house is most graceful with such a basement, for it looks like a thing perfect in itself'. The attic storey was contained within a hipped roof, lit by dormer windows and crowned with a balustrade, tall, panelled chimneystacks and a cupola. Unlike Coleshill, however, the walls were of red brick, and Pratt also added at the centre a three-bay pediment embellished by a marble coat of arms within a cartouche.

The pediment appears again in Pratt's short-lived but immensely influential Clarendon House in Piccadilly (1664–7), the central section of which was an almost exact copy of Kingston Hall. However, in several other respects Clarendon House was unusual, being a town house with flanking wings, and commissioned by Charles II's Lord Chancellor. Pratt built generally for well-educated members of the gentry like Sir Ralph Bankes, who understood the niceties of Classical architecture. They had fewer servants than the aristocratic country-house builders of the previous century and lived in less state, more privately and domestically. The plan that Pratt developed suited admirably their 'politer way of living', as it was described by the diarist John Evelyn, who had befriended Pratt in Rome. He abandoned the traditional central courtyard, thinking it 'stately indeed, but exceeding costly, and only fit for the purses of those who are very rich'. For a 'private man', he considered the best plan to be the 'oblong square' or 'double pile' developed by Jones – that is a straightforward oblong block, comprising two ranges of rooms set back to back. Pratt recommended, 'Let the fairest rooms ... be placed in the very midst of the house, as the bulk of a man is between his members'. At Kingston Hall these were the double-height entrance hall and Great Parlour beyond, with the Great Chamber directly above the latter for formal dining. This arrangement was a throwback to medieval times when servants still dined with the family in the hall, rather than separately in the basement, and the family required another, more private dining-room.

At the four corners of the house on the principal and first floors Pratt placed eight apartments, each consisting of a square, semi-public room adjoining the main reception rooms, and one, or usually two, smaller and more private closets beyond. On either side of the hall were, to the west, the great stairs, which rose only to the first, bedchamber floor, and were used by the family and guests; and, to the east, the great backstairs, which connected the kitchen and other domestic offices in the basement with the

servants' bedrooms in the attic, and were for the servants alone. Pratt was concerned to enforce this social demarcation: 'that the ordinary servants may never publically appear in passing to and fro for their occasions there.' He even worried about where the servants slept: 'Let none . . . be lodged over the strangers' quarters, that they may not disquiet them either by their going to bed late at night, or early rising in the morning.' On both first and second floors, there was a corridor running east-west the length of the house and dividing the two ranges of rooms of Pratt's 'double-pile' plan, as at Coleshill. On the first floor it formed an open gallery, or *pergolo*, at the centre of the house, spanning the south end of the hall and turning this room into a cube; it probably also served to support the north side of the cupola. On the second floor the corridor formed a broader gallery, which recalled Tudor long galleries. During restoration the remains of

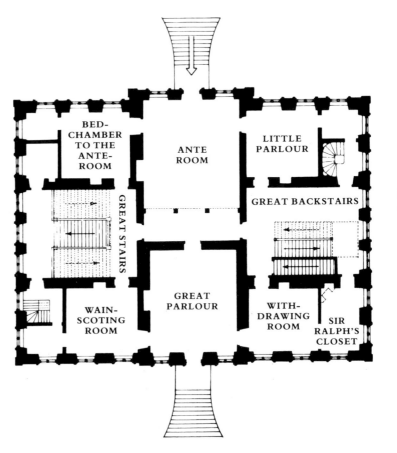

Plan of the principal floor in 1663

James, 1st Duke of Ormonde (1610–88), who spent his last two years at Kingston Hall; by Sir Peter Lely (Kedleston Hall, Derbyshire)

circular niches (later filled in) were revealed in the hall, which probably contained busts, as at Coleshill.

On 9 April 1663 Sir Ralph entered into an agreement with Thomas Fitch of Farnham in Surrey to erect the carcass of the house 'after the most masterly manner that may be'. Fitch was more than simply a master bricklayer, being a central figure in the booming building trade of Restoration London, where he put up for himself a house inspired by Pratt. At Kingston Lacy Fitch acted as clerk of works, choosing as master mason a Mr Goodhew, Giles Hinde, a London stonecutter, and Joseph Godfrey, a mason from Sherborne. Creamy oolitic limestone for the dressings and pediment came from Chilmark quarry eighteen miles away in

Wiltshire at a cost of 10 shillings per ton, with transport a substantial further 16 shillings. The carcass was probably up by October 1665, when Pratt measured the house and noted, as 'cavills', various things that still needed attending to: he was not one 'to spoil a custard to save an egg', as he put it. Fitting out the house followed, which may not have been finished until 1667.

To adorn his new house, Sir Ralph tried in vain to recover some of the sumptuous furnishings of Corfe appropriated by Colonel Bingham, but the latter had sold £1,000 worth of the contents to a London broker who had disposed of much of them to the 2nd Earl of Manchester. It is not clear how Sir Ralph first furnished Kingston Hall, but evidently he was overstretched by its costs. In 1670 he sold his wife's inheritance and the following year placed his own land in the hands of trustees. He was quite seriously in debt by 1675, when he made his will. Remembering the education he and his brothers had received, he made careful provisions for his own sons' education and travel abroad. His other concern was for his collection:

I will that my Study of Bookes, my mapps, my Pictures, my Medailes and other Curiosities and piece of Antiquity shall be reserved for my eldest Son, and not disposed of by my Trustees amongst the rest of the Personall estate towards the payment of debts.

John Bankes was still only twelve when his father died in 1677, and in order to raise money, he was later obliged to let Kingston Lacy. So the house briefly became the home of one of the great figures of the Stuart Court. The 1st Duke of Ormonde had made his reputation in the 1630s fighting in Ireland, which he held for the Crown through the Civil War. He went into exile with Charles II and at the Restoration was created Duke of Ormonde. His great influence made him powerful enemies and he was in and out of favour at Court. By 1686, when he retired to Kingston Lacy, he was an old man in search of a quiet life, and here he died at 78 in 1688.

CHAPTER THREE

THE EIGHTEENTH CENTURY

In 1691 John Bankes (1665–1714) married Margaret, daughter of Sir Henry Parker of Honington, Warwickshire. She brought him useful contacts and some much-needed money, but even more important, proved an outstandingly competent wife, whose surviving portrait as a girl (No. 119) offers little hint of the influence she was to exert over the family's future.

The last £200 of Sir Ralph Bankes's debts were cleared in May 1692, soon after the birth of John, their eldest son, and at Michaelmas 1693 the family returned to live at Kingston Hall. They at once took the management of the estate into their own hands, Margaret herself becoming the effective steward. During the years which followed she produced ten more children, five sons and five daughters, but she never allowed anything to upset her book-keeping. Week after week, for nearly 30 years, she wrote her meticulous entries in four separate account books, striking a balance each Michaelmas and calculating the surplus – or more often the deficit – to be carried forward. Her work was legible and formidably accurate, as it needed to be, since the Bankes family could not afford mistakes. If they were going to survive, they had to live within their means.

Margaret's account of general expenditure, begun at her marriage, records all the purchases made in London during 1693 to refurnish and re-equip Kingston Hall. No inventory detailing the contents of each room at that time has yet been found, but her information on its own is very revealing. To take just one example, no fewer than thirteen beds were acquired, ranging from 'a blew Velvett Bed lined with white damask and embroidered' (at £115 7s the most expensive item of all) to 'a sad colour'd stuf Bed for a garett' at £1 7s. Sheets for these beds did not come ready-made; the raw material was bought in bulk (flax for best, hemp for the servants), then spun into thread and woven up.

There were tables and chairs, silver candlesticks, crockery and pewter plates (at 15s a dozen, 4d apiece extra for engraving), '2 peices of tap'stry hangings for the withdrawing room' for £68 from 'Mr Jones', '19 peices of printed paper to hang two garetts at 3s apeice', and so on – all the multifarious things required to make an empty house habitable and give the important rooms some style.

Very little even of the richest furniture has survived – possibly a mirror and two cabinets, and some of the Delftware. Only the clocks can be identified with any confidence. Two signed by Francis Raynsford, who had a shop at Charing Cross in 1693, must be the two recorded as pur-

John Bankes the Elder (1665–1714); by Thredder, 1702 (No. 114; South-East Bedroom)

chased that summer in London, each costing £12.

These extra expenses ran the family into over £1,200 of debt, and for nearly twenty years money was very tight. Only when the older generation began to die off did resources become available for improvements. Sir Ralph's widow, Mary (d.1711), had little to leave, her inheritance having been sold in 1670, but in the same year his sister Elizabeth ('Aunt Prynce') left £2,300. In the house several stone chimneypieces were installed and three rooms were panelled. It may have been about this time that the *pergolo* was taken down. Work was undertaken in the garden too, probably on schemes which Sir Ralph had not been able to complete. In September 1714, in the midst of these operations, John Bankes was killed at the age of 49, a shadowy figure compared with his father and his wife. He was in the habit of keeping a pistol and a blunderbuss, both loaded, by his bed. One morning, while he was still half-dressed, one of them caught in his dressing-gown and went off, shooting him in the head. But the garden programme was carried through, and Margaret raised the money to send his son and heir, also John, to live in France from 1715 to 1718; from there he visited Italy, thus rounding off an education begun at Winchester and Magdalen College, Oxford.

The family's economic future would have been bleak, with daughters to be found dowries and sons to be launched on careers, all on an income which remained static, had there not been a succession of deaths. Four of the five girls died in childhood, leaving only Mary, who married a baronet, Sir Thomas I'Anson. Five of the boys survived to manhood, but Ralph died at Cambridge, and Charles, a midshipman in the navy, is last recorded embarking for the West Indies. Edward was found a place in the East India Company, and £1,000 of his fortune 'was remitted to him ... in Peices of Eight', to provide capital for trading ventures. But within two years he too was dead. So, apart from John, only Henry was left. Educated at Eton and King's College, Cambridge, he entered Lincoln's Inn and was called to the Bar in 1726, thereafter following a successful career as a barrister.

At Michaelmas 1719, a year after John's return from France, his mother handed over to him and

John Bankes the Younger (1692–1772) as a boy; by Thredder, 1702 (No. 115; South-East Bedroom)

moved to London, where she remarried. John lived at Kingston Hall as a bachelor for the next 52 years. He had occasional flurries of extravagance: a set of sconces and pier-glasses from James Riorto, the London cabinetmaker, in 1726 for £29; a pair of wrought-iron gates from Mr Montigny in 1733 for £11 7s. But for the most part he lived frugally on his estate, a member of the Tory gentry, gradually paying off the debts he had inherited. He was a conscientious, rather unimaginative head of the family.

John's financial position was sound enough by 1730 to refurbish the house. The stonework was cleaned, the windows on the north and south fronts reglazed 'with the best London Crown Glass', and the north court remodelled. George Dowdney was commissioned to paint his portrait (No. 26) and to clean the family collection of pictures. More drastic repairs were forced on him in 1736–8 by the threat of structural collapse. Extra support had to be given to the two staircases by inserting ten wooden columns, and the roof was rebuilt without Pratt's cupola and balustrade.

Kingston Hall, after the roof had been rebuilt by John Bankes the Younger without Pratt's cupola and balustrade; engraving from the Rev. John Hutchins's 'Dorset' (1774)

These details come from the account books, which John dutifully continued after his mother's departure. But he was never so dedicated nor so thorough as Margaret, and in April 1741 he gave up altogether, leaving the blotting paper at the last entry. For the next thirty years a few scraps of paper and a dozen letters are the only records which exist. The likelihood that he was struck down by illness is strengthened by a letter from his friend John Bond, who wrote a few years later, 'You have my warmest wish for the continuance of your recovery.' Yet his self-confidence never seems to have returned. He handed his seat in parliament over to Henry (who held it until appointed Commissioner of Customs in 1762), gave up his position as Lieutenant of Purbeck, and neglected his estates. A story was later passed round the family 'that this Mr John Bankes was such a miser that he always dressed in a long dressing Gown so as to save the expense of trousers and that he saved a large sum of money', none of which was more than half true, but it suggests

that he spent his later years as a somewhat eccentric recluse.

John's lack of decisiveness almost caused a political débâcle. The borough of Corfe Castle returned two MPs, the seats normally being shared, without an election, by a Bankes 'Tory' and a Bond 'Whig'. But from time to time other neighbouring landowners bought up house property in the borough to gain votes and challenge the Bankes/Bond interest. When this happened in 1757, John Bankes failed to take counter-measures. Henry, very worried, wrote from London asking John Bond to call at Kingston Hall to decide a plan of campaign. In his outspoken reply Bond described John as 'supine and negligent', and added that, though he was always ready to call on John, 'I know your Brother's irresolution so well that I am satisfied we should come to no Decisions without your concurrence.' The crisis passed, and thereafter the Bankes family made it their policy to buy up all the house property they could in the borough (which largely explains why the Trust now owns much of Corfe Castle village), but the incident reveals the contrasting characters of the two brothers. John's kindly personal diffidence led, in public affairs, to benign neglect, whereas Henry was driven by the restless ambition of an entrepreneur. Nowhere was this more clearly demonstrated than in the protracted crisis of the black lead mine.

This mine in Borrowdale, Cumberland, of which Sir John Bankes had bought a half-share in 1622, produced high-grade graphite ('black lead') for making pencils and coating moulds used in metal-casting; demand for both of these increased rapidly in the eighteenth century. Every few years the mine was opened and enough graphite extracted to satisfy the market; then it was closed again. But there was a long history of pilfering and smuggling via a network of local receivers, so that little of the profit ever reached the proprietors. Every attempt to put things right was frustrated by the Cumberland mafia, until John Bankes, despairing, suggested selling off the family's half-share.

Henry refused to be defeated. He assumed managerial responsibility himself and tackled the problems with his mother's tenacity. In 1752 he steered an Act through parliament which made receiving black lead a felony, and then transferred

Henry Bankes the Younger (1757–1834); painted in Rome in 1779 by Pompeo Batoni (No. 13; Library)

all sales to London. By manoeuvring the co-proprietor into selling out, he gained a controlling interest for the Bankes family, and when any objectors lodged claims, he fought them in the courts. Alternatively, he cajoled, outfaced or bribed them into compliance. It took him nearly twenty years, but in the end he extended his grip over every side of the business. Until the inventions of the French chemist Nicolas-Jacques Conté destroyed their monopoly in 1815, the Bankes family controlled the only source of pure natural graphite then known. At its peak around 1810, their share brought them £1,500 a year. As early as the 1780s, it was worth £1,000 a year, which provided most of the working capital for the two great projects of that decade, the enclosing of the estate and the rebuilding of the house.

Though already in his seventies, Henry showed the same dynamic efficiency in reorganising the estate when he succeeded John in 1772. Straight-

Henry Bankes the Elder (1698–1776); by George Dowdney, 1734 (No. 32; Drawing Room)

away he negotiated proper contracts with his stewards and put all tenancies on a businesslike footing, giving 30 squatters notice to quit. In 1773 he sold most of the government stock accumulated by himself and John, and bought Shapwick Champayne, the estate next to Kingston Lacy, from the 1st Earl Spencer; the cost was £26,500, more than double what John had spent *in toto* during the previous 50 years on agricultural and house property combined. In the same year he commissioned William Woodward to survey his Dorset estates as a prelude to enclosure. This resulted in two magnificent volumes illustrated with detailed maps, one for the northern properties round Kingston Lacy, the other for Corfe Castle and Purbeck, which Woodward presented with his report in 1775. Henry also initiated the modernising of the house, by employing the Customs Surveyor William Rice to build new offices in the laundry (later the

kitchen) courtyard. All this was done in the last four years of his life, when he was suffering severely from kidney stones. By his exertions he had refounded the family's base; by his second marriage, in 1753, to Margaret Wynne, daughter of the Bishop of Bath and Wells, he formed a union with a cultured and wealthy family, from whom an extra fortune was to accrue to his grandson William.

His son, Henry the Younger (1757–1834), succeeded in 1776 while still up at Cambridge. In 1778 he set off on the Grand Tour and by the following year had reached Rome, where he sat, at his mother's insistence, to Pompeo Batoni, the painter of many English *milordi*. Henry was not impressed with the result (No. 13), as he wrote to his mother on 24 November 1779: 'It is certainly like me, but without any sort of Taste or good painting.' In Rome he also met two young English architectural students from the Royal Academy Schools, John

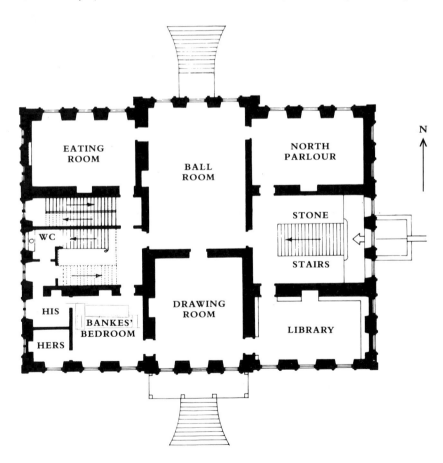

Plan of the principal floor in 1783

Kingston Hall, showing the pergola added by Brettingham to the south front and the new entrance porch on the east front; engraving by J. Smith after J. P. Neale, 1823

Soane and his friend Robert Furze Brettingham. Soane produced two designs, dated 1779, for remodelling Kingston Lacy by adding a full attic storey with a low pitched roof, but nothing came of his scheme. (Bankes was later to be a considerable thorn in Soane's flesh, publicly attacking his designs for the New Law Courts and New State Paper Office in London.) Soane returned to England in 1780, but Brettingham was still in Rome in 1782, when Henry made a second visit and gave him the commission to modernise Kingston Hall. Brettingham wrote back from Rome to his uncle, the architect Matthew Brettingham the Younger, asking him to take the house's measurements, and without yet having seen it, produced a series of designs for remodelling and redecoration. In 1784, shortly after he had returned to England, Henry

married Frances Woodley (No. 29), a noted beauty with a dowry of £6,000. He then set about enclosing the estate and, over the next six years, carrying out Brettingham's proposals for the house.

In accordance with current fashion, the kitchen was moved out of the house into the expanded east end of Rice's office block. To create larger rooms in three of the four corner blocks on the principal floor, Brettingham did away with Pratt's closets and backstairs. The first-floor Great Chamber having been given up as a dining-room, he turned the enlarged room in the north-west corner into a new 'Eating Room'. This was conveniently adjacent to the new kitchen, but was also right next to Pratt's wind-swept entrance. So a new main entrance was made at basement level in the stable yard, then still on the east side. Entering under an Ionic porch, the visitor immediately climbed a new flight of stone stairs to the centre of the house. At the top of the stairs, one could either turn left into the new Library, right into the North Parlour (similarly enlarged), or go straight ahead into the Ballroom, which had been created from the chilly entrance hall by glazing the old front door. Mullioned windows were by then out of date, and sashes were introduced on all except the west elevation facing the kitchen yard. On the south front the sashes were even extended fashionably down to the floor, although the garden level was not raised to meet them. However, a roofed and arcaded pergola was built on to this front to shade the three windows of the central Drawing Room, which replaced Pratt's Great Parlour. In the six years the rebuilding lasted, Frances Bankes had five children, and her husband must have been conscious of the need for more bedrooms in a house that had belonged to a bachelor for most of the century. An additional bedroom was therefore inserted above the stone entrance stairs.

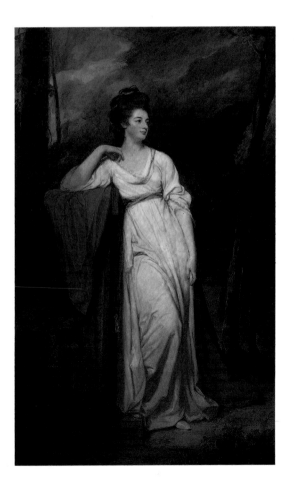

Most of Brettingham's work was swept away by Charles Barry in the 1830s, but one can still get a strong sense of it from the Saloon, which was decorated in the then fashionable manner of James Wyatt with a marble chimneypiece by Flaxman and a coved ceiling painted in 1790 with delicate Neo-classical motifs by Cornelius Dixon. In December 1791 the Bankeses held a ball to celebrate the completion of the rebuilding. Frances described the occasion to her mother-in-law:

The Company ... met about nine, when the Dancing began, (there were thirty six couple) it lasted till one without ceasing, when the Eating Room and North Parlour Doors were opened, and displayed a very handsome Supper ... We contrived to accommodate a hundred and thirty or forty people, who had all full room to sit down. We borrowed all the men servants out of livery in the neighbourhood who were particularly clever and attentive in waiting, and I really believe that not a single Creature had occasion to call twice for any one thing, which is a great deal to say in so large a Company.

After Supper the Dancing began again with great Spirit and lasted till about seven o'clock without any intermission.

Henry Bankes seems to have been equally pleased with his new house, as he did little to it during the following 43 years he lived there. He was MP for Corfe from 1780 and then for Dorset from 1826 to 1831 as a stubborn independent Tory, an opponent of the American War of Independence and friend of the younger Pitt and the Duke of Wellington. Contemporaries regarded him as the spokesman in the Commons for the British Museum, of which he was an active and zealous trustee. He stocked his library with history and the classics, himself publishing *A Civil and Constitutional History of Rome* in 1818. It is not clear how many pictures he added to the collection, but he encouraged his son William, a very different character, whose acquisitions nearly all arrived during his lifetime.

(Left) Frances Woodley (1760–1823), who married Henry Bankes the Younger in 1784; by George Romney, 1780–1 (No. 29; Drawing Room)

BANKES FAMILY TREE

Owners of Kingston Lacy are shown in CAPITALS
Asterisk denotes a portrait in the house

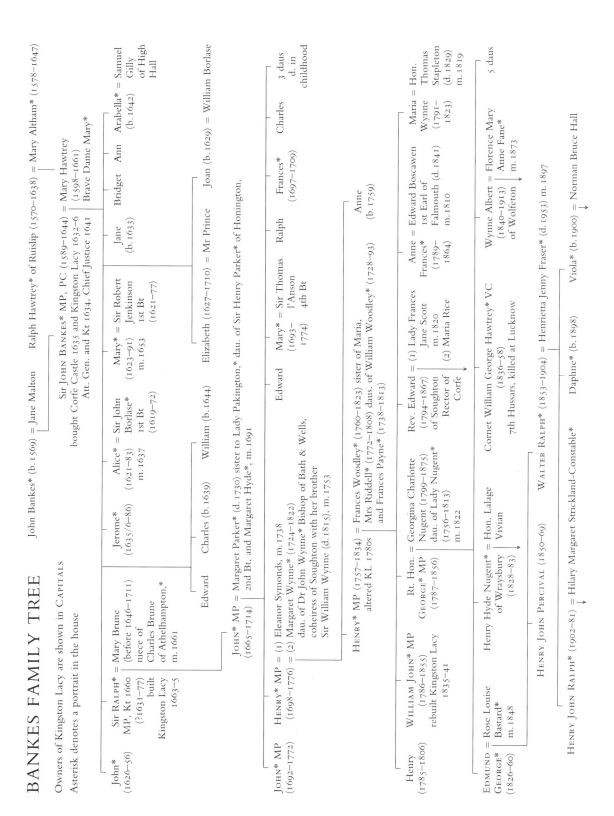

CHAPTER FOUR

WILLIAM BANKES'S TRAVELS IN THE EAST

... all the world is now open to the curiosity of the Traveller.

Sir William Wynne to his heir William Bankes in 1812.

William, Henry's second son, was by far the most original member of the Bankes family. Handsome, conceited and a great talker, he baffled his old-fashioned father, but was doted on by his mother. After Harrow he went up to Trinity College, Cambridge in 1804 where his lifelong friend Lord Byron considered him 'my collegiate pastor, and master, and patron', who 'ruled the Roast – or rather the Roasting – and was father of all mischiefs'. Encouraged by his great-uncle, Sir William Wynne, who sent him books of engravings of English cathedrals, he decorated his rooms in Great Court in the Gothick taste with much Bankes heraldry. In these rooms Byron first read Scott's poetry and William built 'an altar at which he daily burned incense, and frequently had the singing-boys dressed in their surplices to chant services', for which he was half-suspected of Catholic tendencies.

He graduated in 1808, serving as MP for Truro, through his brother-in-law's interest, from 1810 to 1812. His maiden speech, in April 1812, was not a success, floundering according to one observer 'while deep in a rhetorical allusion to the lake of Geneva'. William was one of the leading lights of the 1812 London season, the year of the miniature by Sandars in the Drawing Room and of his rejected proposal to the bluestocking heiress Annabella Milbanke. 'He is very clever, very original and has a fund of information; he is also very good-natured, but he is not much of a flatterer . . .,' wrote Byron. She wrote, 'One of my smiles would encourage him, but I am niggardly of my glances.' At the time she also dismissed Byron's advances, but was finally carried away by the fame he achieved with *Childe Harold* – William had lent her a copy Byron gave

him – and they married in 1815. 'I am afraid he will hear of *us* with pain,' she wrote to Byron, 'yet he cannot *lose* hope, for I never allowed it to exist.'

William had followed in the footsteps of Byron and William Beckford to Portugal and Spain in 1812, where he spent two years acquiring paintings during the disruption of the Peninsular War. He preferred the bohemian life of the gypsies in Granada to that of Wellington's headquarters, which he visited after the Battle of Salamanca in July 1812. If his enthusiasm outstripped his experience in these early years of collecting, he may be counted among the first Englishmen to show an interest in Spanish paintings and he did acquire one masterpiece, the *Holy Family with the infant St John* (No. 42), formerly in Charles I's collection (see Chapter Seven). From Spain he sailed to Alexandria in December 1814 and then to Italy, returning to Egypt in 1815. His travels were to last eight years.

He wrote to his father that he was obliged to travel *'en grand seigneur* . . . I have a noble barge with a cabin'. While waiting for this to be prepared, he visited Mount Sinai in August 1815. Returning to Cairo, he engaged as guide Giovanni Finati, whose *Life and Adventures* he later wrote down and published. Since William's own proposed account of his travels in the East never materialised, it is through Finati that we can follow him. The first journey to upper Egypt and Nubia lasted three months, from September to December 1815, when he recorded the hieroglyphic and Greek inscriptions on a fallen obelisk at Philae and reached beyond the Second Cataract at Wadi Halfa. From January to June 1816 he made his first expedition into Syria, where he drew plans of Djerash, stayed with the great Middle Eastern traveller Lady Hester Stanhope on Mount Lebanon, and eventually with great difficulty managed to cross the desert to Palmyra.

By November 1817 William was back in Syria,

before rejoining Finati in Jerusalem, where they met Captains Irby and Mangles, Thomas Legh of Lyme Park and, briefly, Lord Belmore of Castle Coole (whose homes are both also the property of the National Trust), and carried out clandestine nocturnal excavations. Their 'singular adventures' east of the Dead Sea included a daring expedition to Petra 'in Bedouin Arab dress of the most ordinary description'. William, in the captains' account, 'from his profound knowledge of ancient history, as well as his skill in drawing, was by far the best calculated to go on such an expedition'. They were among the first Europeans to reach Petra.

From October 1818 into the early summer of 1819 he made his second, longer Egyptian expedition, leading Henry Salt's flotilla up the Nile in his fourteen-oared *canjia*. Salt, the British Consul-General, called William 'a most delightful companion, from his extraordinary powers of memory, and the opportunities he has had for observation' and

William John Bankes (1786–1855); miniature by George Sandars, 1812 (Drawing Room)

'high-bred, well informed, and possessing an inexhaustible fund of humour'. The party included Finati, three artists – Henry Beechey (son of the portrait painter), Dr Alessandro Ricci and a young French midshipman, Louis Linant de Bellefonds – and Giovanni Belzoni. Belzoni had begun life performing feats of strength as 'the Patagonian Sampson' on the stage of Sadler's Wells, but went on to become a hydraulic engineer and pioneer excavator of Egyptian antiquities. Bankes set Ricci to copy the wall paintings in the rock tombs at Beni Hasan. His own plan of the great temple at Luxor was made to correct that of the French antiquary Vivant Denon. He also carried out excavations at El-Sebua in Nubia and at Abydos, where he discovered the table of the kings, now in the British Museum.

William engaged Belzoni to bring the Philae obelisk to Kingston Lacy, an operation which lasted twenty years and started inauspiciously when 'the monument plunged endlong into the river almost out of sight'. William produced lithographs of its bilingual inscriptions on his return to England in 1821, which were to play a significant part in unravelling the mystery of Egyptian hieroglyphics. He published little else, as he explained to Byron in 1822: 'I am always thinking of it, and, from a strange mixture of indolence with industry always deferring it. I hate, and always did, method and arrangement, and this is what my materials want.'

Bankes's party spent a month at Abu Simbel where the great temple of Rameses II, discovered by the Swiss traveller Johann Burckhardt in 1813 almost engulfed in sand, had been opened by Belzoni and Finati, with Irby and Mangles, the year before. They uncovered with difficulty one of the colossal figures of the façade where William discovered a Greek inscription that helped to date the monument. Inside the temple they worked up ladders, half-naked and in great heat, to copy all the wall paintings by the light of candles. Many of these coloured drawings are still in pristine condition among the Bankes MSS at Kingston Lacy. The 24-year-old architect Charles Barry encountered the party in January 1819. From their first meeting Barry, himself already a skilled draughtsman, admired William's 'brilliancy and talent'.

Rameses II before three gods; wall painting at Abu Simbel, copied by Linant de Bellefonds for William Bankes

William nearly reached Dongola before being obliged by the threat of war in Nubia to return to Cairo, but commissioned Linant to continue on to Meroë and to record the antiquities of Nubia. Linant's drawings constitute an invaluable record of many sites since damaged or destroyed and, afterwards engaged by the African Society, he devoted the rest of his long life to Egypt as a geographer and engineer, accepting the title of Pasha in 1873. The Billiards Room now displays William Bankes's Egyptian antiquities and a small changing selection of the drawings made by himself and by the several artists he commissioned (see p.81).

If William was passionately intent to unearth and record the ancient monuments of Egypt in the early amateur days before much was known about Egyptian culture, he does not seem to have collected at all systematically. His classical education and observant eye enabled him to acquire manuscripts and papyri, but he appears to have made little effort to integrate his antiquities into his rebuilding of Kingston Lacy from the 1830s to '40s. Nor did he enlarge his collection much at that time, when important antiquities were for sale in London. His only known later acquisitions were the granite sarcophagus of Amenomope on the south lawn (see Chapter Nine), given to him by Henry Salt in 1822, and the remarkable Roman bust of green basalt acquired in 1828, once thought to be of Mark Anthony.

In 1819 William left Egypt for Venice and spent the winter there with Byron, purchasing the *Judgement of Solomon* (No. 33), Velázquez's *Cardinal Massimi* (No. 101) and other remarkable pictures in Bologna early in 1820. In February he was in Florence, where, not surprisingly, he felt the cold. He visited Byron for the last time in Ravenna, and they 'buffooned together very merrily', before joining his sister Maria in Rome in March. 'How he will bear the gift of a Roman *coat* with his Asiatic ideas, I have no conception', noted his mother when she received her daughter's letter. His reputation as 'the Nubian explorer' who 'has done *miracles* of research and enterprize' (in Byron's words) preceded his return home in April 1820.

From the journal of the society hostess Mrs Arbuthnot, who became a close friend, we learn that 'the great traveller', who in June 1821 'was

The Philae obelisk on the south lawn

excessively entertaining and told us many stories of his travels', was lionised by society. Indeed, the normally hostile Samuel Rogers in his *Table Talk* said, 'Witty as Sidney Smith was, I have seen him at my own house absolutely overpowered by the superior facetiousness of William Bankes'. In June 1822 Mrs Arbuthnot helped to dissuade William from pursuing his affair with the young and pretty but unhappy Lady Buckinghamshire who, desperately in love with William, was 'excessively anxious to induce Mr Bankes to go off with her and to take her with him disguised as a boy into Africa, where he has some thoughts of going', to find the sources of the Nile. William was not finished with travelling, but the next two decades were to be devoted to his British inheritance.

CHAPTER FIVE

WILLIAM BANKES AND KINGSTON LACY

Who ever could say of the Arts with more truth than I can *Res secundas ornant, in adversis solatium et perfugium praebent.**

William Bankes to his brother George, May 1844.

William had a passion for architecture and the means to indulge it. He had become heir to the Kingston Lacy estates in 1806 on the death of his elder brother Henry, who had been shipwrecked *en route* for Sicily and, with typical Bankes obstinacy, refused to take to the lifeboat. Even during his father's lifetime, William was receiving £8,000 a year, and in 1815 he also inherited Soughton in Flintshire, the eighteenth-century house of his great-grandfather, Bishop Wynne. On his return from Egypt in 1820 he immediately set about rebuilding it. The somewhat eccentric result, alas much altered in the 1860s, was a collaboration

between Bankes and Charles Barry, although Bankes seems to have been largely his own architect. Giovanni Finati paid a visit in 1823 and has left an account of Soughton:

The house at first sight reminded me much ... of some of the old villas in the north of Italy, ... for it has towers and much ornamented stone-work and walled courts about it, and lines of trees in almost all directions; and instead of that trim and compact appearance in the inside which English houses generally present, (especially in London,) there are here large open chambers and galleries, very lofty, but quite naked of furniture, and with little else but the bare walls. The whole was, however, then under repair or rebuilding, and a great deal of it quite unfinished.

When the work was finished, Soughton was further embellished with Gobelins tapestries and a Rubens cartoon of *The Triumph of Divine Love*. As William

Soughton Hall in Flintshire, which William Bankes inherited in 1815; lithograph by N. Whittock

* 'Art is the ornament of good times and a consolation in bad times', misquoted from Cicero, *pro Archia*, 7.16.

Elevation of the south front of Charles Barry's house, 'drawn by candlelight' in 1849 by Seymour, the clerk of works

wrote to his mother about the place, 'There will be few prettier in this part of Wales.'

Even before he returned from the East, William seems to have begun pestering his father to make changes to Kingston Hall. In 1819 Thomas Cundy junior submitted three schemes for remodelling the interior, principally to create a larger dining-room. Two years later Henry Bankes called in Jeffry Wyatt, who produced a similar, somewhat clumsy proposal. All were rejected by Henry, but William persisted, writing to his father in 1821 about Charles Barry:

... He is a very nice architectural draughtsman and therefore when I move into Dorsetshire I will have him down to Kingston Hall in order to have exact elevations and plans made of those alterations there which I have only roughly sketched upon paper, as well as to set him to contriving the distribution above the stairs; that, whether executed or not, there may remain in evidence what were my notions upon the subject as confronted with those of Wyatt.

There the matter rested until Henry Bankes died in December 1834, when William was at last free to start remodelling Kingston Hall as he wished. Years

later he described his feelings about the old house he had inherited:

The house had continued to the third generation quite unaltered but the naturally timid disposition of my great uncle John Bankes induced him to remove the lantern altogether ... It came into my father's hands with no greater alterations than these and had it passed through his hands intact as it came into them I might have hesitated long about permitting myself to make any considerable change. It would have been interesting as a very complete and handsome specimen of the period and there were features in it that coupled with that impression that antiquity gives could not have failed to strike both as in themselves grand and as pictures of the life and manners of their days. The Great Hall especially with its Music Gallery and the broad staircase ... would have been some palliative for present incommodiousness which I thought inadmissible in an altered house that was neither old nor modern in its character but a bad mixture of both.

William belonged to the Romantic generation that had been inspired by Fonthill, William Beckford's picturesque fantasy house in Wiltshire, which he had visited in secret as a young man. Had he inherited sooner, he might have decided to rebuild

Corfe as the family seat in the same spirit. But the Gothick undergraduate of thirty years before, the amateur architect of Soughton, had become by the mid-1830s a true amateur of architecture. His passion was now for the Italian *palazzi* that had inspired Inigo Jones and Roger Pratt in the seventeenth century, and Charles Barry again in the 1830s, when he created the Travellers' Club in Pall Mall, of which William was, naturally, a member.

So in 1835 William called in Barry once again, and over the next six years they together transformed Kingston Hall. Although Barry was by the 1830s the most successful architect in Britain, William, who was not an easy client, kept him on a short rein, insisting on many ideas of his own, which he followed through in the greatest detail. He had two principal aims: firstly, to restore the house in the manner of Inigo Jones, whom he supposed was Sir Ralph's architect; secondly, to make it more convenient for modern life. So the house was encased entirely in Chilmark stone, a new balustrade, cupola and dormers placed on the roof to replace those removed in the eighteenth century, and tall chimneystacks resembling those at Coleshill, then also thought to be by Jones, added at the corners.

The entrance was moved back to the north front, but instead of being up a set of stairs into the *piano nobile*, the ground on this side of the house was lowered eight feet to accommodate a new *porte-cochère* at basement level. Guests would then be able to alight from their carriages out of the rain and enter the house through a new basement Entrance Hall, which would also reduce draughts in the main rooms. This idea was borrowed from Amesbury Abbey in Wiltshire, also attributed to Jones at that time. On the south front, Brettingham's pergola was removed, and a balustraded terrace, based on that at the Queen's House, added along the length of the house at principal-floor level. This provided more dignified access from the house to the garden, and also masked the basement windows and consequently the servants' view of the garden. For the east front Barry designed a loggia heavily banded and rusticated in the style of the Watergate at York House in London, another building given

The Marble Staircase

to Jones. A double staircase descends from it into the garden. The internal decoration of the house also borrowed from or was inspired by Jonesian buildings which William or Barry had studied at first hand. So, for instance, the new plasterwork ceilings in the Drawing Room, Dressing Room and Dining Room were modelled on those at Lees Court in Kent, the Queen's House and Coleshill respectively.

William set out thirteen good practical reasons why it was necessary to replan the interior. As had been acknowledged for two generations, Brettingham's dining-room at the north-west corner of the house was too small. He overcame the problem, at some disturbance to the structure, by removing the partition between the south-west apartment and Brettingham's west stairs, and by raising the ceiling of the large new room created. At the same time he raised the ceiling of the adjoining Drawing Room, which he thought too low by comparison with the Ballroom. There was only one watercloset, so he added more. After Brettingham's remodelling, the only access to the bedroom floor for those coming in with muddy boots was across the Ballroom carpet and up the west stairs, which had a disagreeable view over the kitchen courtyard. William's solution, a staircase of Carrara marble, is a *tour de force*. Replacing Brettingham's stone stairs, it linked the new Entrance Hall in the basement directly with the bedroom floor in a series of vistas that cleverly used false perspective to increase the Baroque sense of space and grandeur. In his profuse notes he wrote:

My recollections of Rome gave the Ruspoli staircase [by the architect Martino Longhi the Younger] a preference over all other staircases that I had seen and this I had so strongly in my mind when I described what I wished to Mr Barry that I sent to Rome for a measured plan and section of it.

He wrote to his brother George in December 1837:

I am astonished at the rate of progress of the works, and more than ever pleased with them, the Lantern is everything that I could wish, and so is the drawing room ceiling, that is to say their effect is exactly what it was upon paper – but the staircase turns out *far beyond* it (if staircase it may be called that stairs has none), it is now formed and roughed out in almost every part, all the openings clear, and all the ceilings shaped so that proportions, and perspectives and distribution, and lighting, can all be judged of quite as well as can ever be, and I must pronounce (though it cannot be said *impartially*) that so far as my judgement goes, there is no staircase in England equal to it in effect, not even Wardour, and not many that surpass it in Italy. I delight in the rich Eastern external Loggia which is finished, but I do nothing but walk up and down the inclined planes of the Staircase.

William was not to enjoy his new staircase for long. In September 1841 he was accused of 'indecently exposing himself with a soldier of the Foot Guards in Green Park'. In 1833 a similar charge had been dropped only after the intervention of the Duke of Wellington and other influential friends. Now he jumped bail and fled to Italy. His affairs were administered by his brother George and his brother-in-law Lord Falmouth, but he retained his financial independence and so had the means to continue commissioning works of art to fit out the interiors of the newly christened Kingston Lacy and to furnish the house. This remained his consuming passion up to the moment of his death fourteen years later. Having little faith in his brother ('George is but a poor judge in art and has but

an indifferent eye'), he turned instead to his sister, Lady Falmouth, who came to stay periodically at Kingston Lacy as a widow from 1841, to oversee the decoration.

Perhaps William's greatest achievement was the Spanish Room, created painstakingly between 1838 and his death in 1855. With a new, larger Dining Room, he no longer needed Brettingham's 'Eating Room' and so he set about transforming the north-west apartment into a harmonious setting for the Spanish paintings he had collected in his youth. First

A piping cherub from one of the boxwood doors in the Dining Room. The figure was taken from Donatello's High Altar in the Santo at Padua

came the magnificent gilded ceiling, which had probably been taken from Scamozzi's Palazzo Contarini degli Scrigni in Venice, and was put up, after a little modification to make it fit, in 1838. The tooled, painted and gilded leather wall-hangings were from another palazzo, and were shipped over in 1853 with detailed instructions from William about how they should be put up. He devoted even greater care to designing the painted doors. 'They bear and require minute examination from their extreme finish; being twelve in number, they represent the months of the year – six upon gold, as the summer months, and six upon bronze as the winter,' he wrote to his sister in 1851. Florentine *pietra dura* panels and gilded sconces completed an interior that had few equals for sumptuousness in mid-nineteenth-century Britain.

There were other consolations in William's Venetian exile; his love of marble became an expertise and he developed into a generous patron of modern art. The *Foglio de Verona* spoke of 'this liberal Englishman who instead of trafficking in the immortal old works of art of Italy trains and encourages and commissions for rising artists'.

William provided designs for Italian craftsmen such as Salesio Pegrassi, the sculptor of the tables in the Entrance Hall and of much of the *Biancone* marble used for carved doorways and candelabra throughout the house. He also chose the models, from admired Renaissance sculptors such as Donatello and della Robbia, for the boxwood doors exquisitely carved by Vincenzo Favenza between 1849 and 1853. The doors were put up in the new Dining Room, but the rest of his scheme for this room was not realised. He also abandoned plans to raise the ceiling of the Library and to embellish it with paintings, in this case to please his sister. He wrote to Lady Falmouth in May 1854:

As I am continually thinking of you, and having so few objects left, my desire is to make you comfortable, and your residence at Kingston Lacy more and more acceptable to you ... I have therefore at once decided on counter ordering it all, and can assure you in all sincerity that I feel more actual pleasure and satisfaction in doing so from such a motive, ... than I could possibly have felt from carrying out my plans.

Perhaps by this stage William felt that he could best enjoy Kingston Lacy vicariously through his sister. However, there is a family story that he paid brief secret visits back to the house on which he had lavished such care. As the family might have been prosecuted for having harboured a fugitive from justice, the papers were carefully doctored after his death, but evidence remains which proves the old story to be true: more than once in 1854, when he knew he was mortally ill, he visited Kingston Lacy clandestinely. It must have given him immense satisfaction to stand again in his beloved family house and to see at first hand the lavish schemes which he had hitherto created only in his mind's eye.

(Left) Anne, Lady Falmouth (1789–1864), William Bankes's sister, who came to stay at Kingston Lacy in 1841; painted by Sir Thomas Lawrence (No. 23; Drawing Room)

CHAPTER SIX

RECENT HISTORY

George Bankes (1787–1856), who looked after the family estates during William's fourteen-year absence, was different in almost every respect from his elder brother. Sensible and cautious, he tried, without success, to rein in William's extravagance. In deference to his mother's wishes, he married an heiress, Georgina Charlotte Nugent, the illegitimate daughter of the Duke of Cumberland, the fifth son of George III and, from 1837, King of Hanover. George shared his father's independent High Tory politics. As MP for Cambridge, he implacably opposed the Catholic Emancipation Bill of 1829 and the Great Reform Bill of 1832, which swept away the rotten borough of Corfe that returned his father. Perhaps because of his distaste at what his brother was doing to Kingston Lacy, which became the domain of his widowed sister Lady Falmouth from 1841, he preferred to live on the family's Corfe estates, building for himself at Studland the Manor House, a substantial villa beside the sea. After the family lost their Corfe parliamentary seat, he was also three times mayor of the town and wrote a history of the castle in 1853. Two years later, at the age of 68, George finally inherited the Bankes estates of which he had been such a careful steward, but his reign was brief, as he died the following year. Characteristically, he chose to be buried, not beside his brother in the family vault in Wimborne, but in the little Norman church at Studland.

Georgina Bankes produced numerous children, but no fewer than six died in infancy. The most famous of those that survived was her third son, William. As a young cornet he served with the 7th Hussars during the Indian Mutiny. On 19 March 1858 he twice charged the enemy until, with his revolver empty, he was cut down. He endured his

hideous wounds with cheerfulness. 'They tell me if I get over this I can go yachting. We'll have some jolly cruises together,' he told William Russell, *The Times*'s famous war correspondent. But eighteen days later he was dead. For his bravery he received the Victoria Cross and was commemorated by a stained-glass window in Studland church.

Between 1856 and 1869 the estate was dogged by a series of premature deaths. Cornet Bankes's eldest brother, Edmund, inherited at the age of 30, but outlived his father by only four years, leaving two sons on his death in 1860. The elder, Henry, was only ten and died unmarried nine years later in 1869.

(Right) Georgina Bankes (1799–1875) with her three eldest children; miniature by Sir William Ross, 1830

So the younger son, Walter Ralph (1853–1904), succeeded, bringing stability to the estate over the following 35 years. An avid horseman, huntsman and gardener, he oversaw numerous changes to the house, garden and park. Although plans he commissioned for a new billiard-room, conservatory and servants' quarters were never realised, a new stable block designed by T. H. Wyatt was erected west of the house in 1880. He also installed electricity in the house in 1885 and telephones in 1889 – both then very novel inventions.

Despite being a valuable catch, Walter Bankes was still a bachelor by his early forties. As his daughter Viola later wrote:

His broad-shouldered figure and aquiline features were as well known in the opera houses of Italy and ballrooms of Paris as in the fields and woods of Dorset. Experience had matured him and his brooding eyes suggested a dangerous sophistication, which contrasted irresistibly with the open smiles of younger men.

In 1897 at the age of 44 he finally married. His bride was Henrietta Jenny Fraser, a famous beauty of Scots-Dutch descent with large hazel eyes and a

*(Above)
Walter Ralph Bankes
(1853–1904), who
inherited Kingston
Lacy in 1869*

*(Left)
Henrietta Fraser,
who married Walter
Bankes in 1897
and ran the Kingston
Lacy estate between
1904 and 1923*

The Drawing Room, photographed in 1900 by 'The Ladies' Field'

fashionably wasp-waisted figure. After two daughters, Daphne and Viola, their long-awaited son, Henry John Ralph, was born in 1902 to much rejoicing on the estate. After that the marriage seems to have cooled. The sophisticated bachelor became a taciturn husband, who gave up socialising in their London home in Wilton Crescent for more solitary country pursuits at Kingston Lacy. By the time of his death in 1904 Walter was communicating with the servants mainly through written notes.

His widow was courted by several neighbours, but never remarried, preferring to devote herself to keeping the estate in order during young Ralph's

minority. She later published an account of the principal events at Kingston Lacy between 1904 and 1923. Her book records a visit in 1905 by Edward VII: he sprained his ankle in a rabbit hole and had to be conveyed to the tree-planting ceremony on the south lawn in a pony chaise. Other royal visitors included Kaiser Wilhelm II in 1907 and the future Queen Mary in 1908. Summers were spent at one of the family's several houses at Studland, playing tennis or walking on the beach; the Manor House eventually became Mrs Bankes's dower house, after Ralph came of age. Christmas was always at Kingston Lacy, where the jardinières in the Drawing Room and Saloon would be filled with brightly coloured hot-house plants before the family awoke on Christmas morning.

In the house Mrs Bankes's tastes are best seen in the White Bedroom and the Drawing Room. She re-covered the walls of the latter with rose damask in 1898 and filled the room with nineteenth-century French furniture and Dresden china, both much favoured in the Edwardian period. After an unsatisfactory report from the sanitary inspector, she oversaw the installation of a new plumbing system in 1909, including four new baths and six lavatories.

Working from her desk in the Library, with the help of the agent, Alfred Lodder, she supervised numerous improvements to the estate. In the kitchen garden new greenhouses went up, from which the head gardener, Mr Hill, produced exotic flowers to decorate the house and soft fruit out of season. In the park she built the church in 1907 with money left for the purpose by her husband and added new entrance lodges in 1912–13. The many cottages and farms improved and extended during this period still bear prominent date blocks marked 'HRB', the initials of the young squire. In the midst of these improvements, all but the most necessary work ceased between 1914 and 1919, while many estate workers left to fight in the Great War. Few of those who joined the Dorset Yeomanry and served at Gallipoli returned.

Mrs Bankes expected her children to marry as well as she had done. In 1935 Ralph married Hilary Strickland-Constable, from an old Yorkshire family, but when his elder sister Viola wed an Australian doctor without her mother's permission, she was effectively banished from the estate. In later years Mrs Bankes preferred to live in Brook Street in London, where she died in 1953, 49 years after her husband.

Under Ralph Bankes, who inherited his father's solitary streak, Kingston Lacy gradually subsided into tranquil decay. During the Second World War the east side of the park was disfigured by a 1,300-bed red-brick military hospital, and the flower garden was turned over to vegetables. In the post-war years the house became one of the most private in Britain, and the superb collection of paintings it contained was rarely seen. So it came as a great surprise when Ralph Bankes bequeathed Corfe and Kingston Lacy to the National Trust in 1981, one of the most generous gifts in its history.

The house the Trust inherited was suffering from major structural problems, which entailed a costly two-year programme of work. Precariously sagging beams had to be strengthened with steel, stonework repaired and the huge roof completely releaded. Rampant dry rot had to be eradicated and many of the delicate contents required conservation. In 1986 the house was ready to receive visitors and continues as the heart of a traditional Dorset estate.

(Left) Ralph Bankes, the donor of Kingston Lacy

CHAPTER SEVEN

THE PAINTINGS AND SCULPTURE

Kingston Lacy has perhaps the oldest established gentry collection of paintings in Britain, many of which can be traced back to lists compiled in the 1650s. The Spanish Room represents a unique assemblage from a school of painting little collected in Britain, in a specially conceived setting, in which the place of each and every picture was carefully planned. The whole collection is also exceptional amongst those in country houses in Britain in being substantially intact.

The beginnings of the collection are modest enough. A list of *c.*1656, recently discovered in a commonplace book of Ralph Bankes's and headed 'Pictures in my Chamber att Grayes Inne', contains just fifteen items. The three still certainly identifiable represent strands that were to run right through Ralph Bankes's collecting: a love of portraiture ('*My Brother and S*^r *Maurice williams*'; No. 133); admiration for Peter Lely ('*Magdalen by m*^r *Lilly*'; No. 58); and a fondness for genre subjects ('*A Night peice of A man A drinking*'; No. 41).

Ralph's second list, probably of 1658, contains eighteen pictures, eleven of which are still certainly identifiable at Kingston Lacy. This list also makes clear Lely's role in forming the collection. He is represented by two autograph pictures, the *Magdalen* (No. 58) and a portrait of *N. Wray* (No. 61), but also by a copy by this same Wray of his *Lady Newport* (No. 130) in the Clarendon Collection. But he is also described as the owner of the original Dou of the '*Man & Woman singing, Night peice on A small board*' (No. 49). Furthermore, Lely was the supplier – and perhaps even the go-between for the commissioning – of the exceptionally sized '*very large lanskip of Berkams*' (No. 69), which, though signed and dated 1655, does not seem to have arrived until 1658.

Ralph Bankes's third and final list is the most interesting of all. Titled and precisely dated: 'A noate of my Pictures att Grayes Inn & w^t thay cost. X^{ber} ye 23rd 1659', it contains 37 pictures and miniatures, with a total value of £363, and the names of those from whom they had been bought. Twenty-one of these pictures are certainly, and another two or three possibly, still identifiable at Kingston Lacy today. A briefer attached list of the same pictures, titled 'The Value of my pictures', adds up to £536 6s – an interesting early example of picture-collecting regarded as profitable investment. This is, unfortunately, the last list or inventory of Sir Ralph Bankes's pictures that we have. His most significant later addition was the remarkable set of portraits by Lely. Long thought to have simply been portraits of Sir Ralph's relations, they in fact depict a much diverser range of sitters, so that it seems unlikely that they were all commissioned by him; it is much more probable that he somehow prevailed upon some of the sitters or the artist to surrender their portraits to him. Sir Ralph's extensive previous dealings with Lely may have burgeoned into friendship, which could also account for his possession of the superb and prime original of a notoriously libertine peeress, *Lady Cullen* (No. 4), when he did not even obtain from Lely a portrait of his own wife. Another explanation is of course conceivable!

Although for over a century Sir Ralph's successors seem to have added nothing but portraits to the collection, they do at least appear to have regarded it as an heirloom, to be passed on with Kingston Hall itself. Even John Bankes the Younger, who only had himself painted by the dimmest of country painters (Nos 10, 26, 109), at least got George Dowdney to restore the whole collection in 1731. In his later years, however, he seems to have let everything run to seed, and it was his brother and successor, Henry, who compiled the first catalogue of the collection, in 1762–4; another followed, when Henry suc-

Landscape with herdsmen; by Nicolaes Berchem, 1655 (No. 69; Saloon); bought by Sir Ralph Bankes through his friend, the painter Peter Lely

The Woodley Family; by Johan Zoffany, c.1766
(No. 118; South-East Bedroom)

ceeded in 1772, and a revised edition of the 1762–4 catalogue in 1775. It was probably also Henry who had so many of the pictures framed or reframed, probably by local craftsmen, and often with imitations of the superb seventeenth-century 'Sunderland' frames on Sir Ralph's Lelys. These are the first such historicising frames dating from the eighteenth century to have been identified anywhere.

Henry's son, also called Henry, appears to have been more interested in collecting prints and drawings than paintings, but he appreciated good English portraiture, and may have ensured that some choice examples found their way to Kingston Hall. He was painted in Rome in 1779 by Batoni (No. 13), 'but to speak without prejudice, I do not think his portraits equal to those of Reynolds.' He also told his mother: 'I hear Angelica [Kauffmann] has left England for Rome – Batoni would find in her a formidable

Rival.' Curiously, he was never painted by Reynolds or Kauffmann, whilst the superb whole-length of his wife, Frances Woodley, by Romney (No. 29), was painted before their marriage. However, it may have been more than just family ties that account for the fact that Reynolds's lovely early portrait of Frances Woodley's mother (No. 22) ended up at Kingston Lacy, as did the fine Lawrence of her sister, *Maria, Mrs Riddell* (No. 28), and the Zoffany of the whole *Woodley Family* (No. 118). Henry evidently took some interest in Old Master paintings as well: he bought a copy of Raphael's *Martyrdom of St Stephen* (No. 67) as a reputed Domenichino from the Barberini Palace in Rome; his son William also sent him detailed explanations of what he had bought in Spain. William sometimes makes it sound as if he was buying the pictures for his father. He certainly counted upon their being hung at Kingston Hall.

William John Bankes was a throwback to Sir Ralph Bankes. In his choice of paintings, he could sometimes be led astray by the resonance of a name, and seems always to have regarded them as much as components of some greater scheme as works of art in their own right. None the less his taste was distinctive and well-defined, impervious to the fashion of the moment; he knew exactly what he wanted, and he generally got it. Kingston Lacy and its contents as we see them today are essentially his creation. In 1824 William spelt out the principles that guided his collecting:

I have always preferred, even in the works of the greatest masters, what is legendary to what is purely historical; that is, I mean, such subjects as admit of light, & angels, & concerts in the clouds &c.; & if you will recollect there are few of the most acknowledged masterpieces that do not contain matters of this sort in them.... The best classical subjects are equally out of nature or above it.... Rubens seems to have been [particularly] sensible of this preference to be given to ideal subjects over plain every day matter of fact.... it is my firm belief that a Protestant country will never produce an historical painter of a high class.

He rejected the naturalistic and the trivial – whether in the form of Dutch realism, English literalism or French frivolity – and some genres, such as landscape or still-lifes, altogether.

Essentially, William had two bouts as a collector of paintings, on both occasions exploiting the experience and opportunities of travel. The first was during his journeys in Spain in 1812-15, when he put together the first collection of Spanish paintings to reach this country to have been formed by someone who had not been a resident of the place. The second was after his Near Eastern interlude, when he returned via Italy in 1819–20, making by far his most important set of purchases altogether in Bologna.

William's collecting in Spain might have begun as sheer opportunism. There he was, already interested in art, one of the first English civilians in a freshly liberated country, in which earlier native works of art were seriously in circulation for the first time, after religious houses had been dissolved by the French, who had carried off some of the best spoils, but had still left rich pickings behind.

He rapidly set himself the task of forming a representative collection of what he justly saw as the golden age of Spanish painting. There is no absolute masterpiece amongst the Spanish pictures he collected in Spain, and many of his swans turned out to be geese – if still geese of respectable pedigree. Others, though of considerable quality, continue to perplex: for example, the *St Augustine* apparently given by Emmanuel Philibert of Savoy to Placencia Cathedral, and successively attributed to Ribera, Murillo and Zurbaran (No. 90). The prize acquisition was actually an Italian work, the *Holy Family* from the circle of Raphael (No. 42). While somehow living in disguise in Pamplona during the English siege of the city in 1813, he dined with the French commander, 'who regaled him with a meal of rats washed down with strong drink'. To buy the Raphael from his host, he was obliged to accept a

The Holy Family; from the circle of Raphael (No. 42; Saloon). It was bought in Spain in 1813 by William Bankes, who commissioned the frame, which includes portraits of Raphael (top) and the supposed former owners of the painting

donkey with it. When he shipped the Raphael and donkey home, the captain declared that 'the jackass should pay, like a gentleman'. Bankes dined out on the story for years after.

William's two finest Spanish pictures were not bought in Spain at all. Velázquez's head-and-shoulders of *Cardinal Massimi* (No. 101) came to him through the break-up of a collection formed under the auspices of the Napoleonic empire, Marescalchi's in Bologna. Ferdinando, Count Marescalchi (1754–1816) had been Foreign Minister of the Cisalpine Republic, and then of the Kingdom of Italy, which essentially meant that he was a high official of the Napoleonic Euro-state. No doubt exploiting this position, he had put together a notable collection of paintings, many of them from Venice, but also from Rome and elsewhere. From his collection also came William's single greatest purchase, the *Judgement of Solomon* (No. 33), then universally ascribed to Giorgione, but now clearly seen to be by Sebastiano del Piombo. Byron was moved to urge a wavering Bankes to buy it:

I know nothing of pictures myself, and care almost as little: but to me there are none like the Venetian – above all, Giorgione. I remember well his Judgement of Solomon in the Mariscalchi in Bologna. The real mother is beautiful, exquisitely beautiful. Buy her, by all means, if you can, and take her home with you.

Bankes's father, by contrast, was appalled at news of the purchase.

When William returned to England in 1820, he needed to instal his purchases. Although his father was still alive, William knew that Kingston Hall was entailed on him, and he always seems to have envisaged them hanging there. Hence his plan for hanging the best of his Spanish pictures in the then North Parlour, which is striking visual evidence of the way in which he already saw his pictures in terms of overall schemes.

William does not seem to have continued to collect pictures in any consistent way after his return to England. However, at the 1827 sale of Count Altamira's collection he bought his second great Spanish picture, Velázquez's whole-length of *Philip IV* (now in the Isabella Stewart Gardner Museum in Boston), and a pair of large animal hunts by Snyders (Nos 105 and 106). The latter had previously been

Cardinal Camillo Massimi; by Velázquez (No. 101; Spanish Room)

seized by the French under Napoleon and sent to the Gobelins to serve as models for tapestries. In acquiring them, William may also have had decorative uses in view; certainly, their ultimate fate was to have their tops folded over and to be made into inset pictures at the top of the stairs. He gave 'Provision for two large Snyder pictures' in the Dining Room as one of the thirteen reasons for altering Kingston Lacy in his notebooks of 1836–40. Similarly, in 1839 he bought from some London dealers an entire ceiling reputedly taken out of the Palazzo Contarini degli Scrigni in Venice, which included paintings that were claimed to be by Veronese and Pordenone, for adaptation to the ceiling of the Eating Room, later the Golden, or Spanish, Room.

This preoccupation with paintings for ceilings or other decorative purposes became even more intense after William was forced into exile in September 1841, when the use of his imagination to transform Kingston Lacy, by remote control from afar, became his governing obsession. Almost immediately, he seems to have bought Reni's early fresco of *Dawn separating Night from Day*, which in 1840 had been taken down from the ceiling of a room in the Palazzo Zani in Bologna and transferred to canvas. This he seems to have wanted placed in the central oval of the Dining Room ceiling. The family later found this unsatisfactory, and transferred it to the ceiling of the Library, where it was much too close to the spectator and took up too much of the surface. Taken down from there by the National Trust, it still awaits restoration, to remedy the effects of its botched transfer from plaster to canvas.

William purchased three more ceilings, or elements of ceilings, in Venice. In 1849 he profited from the crisis in confidence caused by the siege of Venice to obtain from the Palazzo Grimani by S. Maria Formosa an entire ceiling, reputed to be 'a joint production of Giorgione and his then scholar John of Udine'. The central octagon, with an illusionistic depiction of putti amongst a trelliswork cupola of vines, was placed over the summit of the main stairs, and the remaining elements were intended for the State Bedroom ceiling, but were evidently found to be mostly unusable and thrown away. The other old elements in the State Bedroom ceiling, three of which William believed to be by Veronese, and the fourth by Padovanino, appear to have come from the *casa-palazzo* Castelli by S. Maria dei Miracoli. He commissioned a painter, Francesco Vason, to make detailed designs 'in the Lombard style' for the ceilings of the State Bedroom and the Library, to incorporate his acquisitions, and to paint or restore the ornamental panels to make up the wholes. The carved wood settings were commissioned from Costante Traversi, 'also part new and part restoration'. The ceiling over the Library had been countermanded, and that over the State Bedroom was still unfinished, when Bankes died; the carved setting of the latter was then evidently also countermanded, and the exisiting ceiling is visibly a botched-up job.

Nothing has been said so far about sculpture, because there was scarcely any of significance at Kingston Lacy before William's time. It was probably when he was living in exile in Venice that he bought many of the old bronzes now at Kingston

Lacy – most notably the Venetian Cinquecento firedogs. It was in Venice too that he found a sculptor, Angelo Giordani, who was able both to carve Venetian well-heads in imitation of ancient models, and to cast such things as bronze doorknockers and handles from Venetian Renaissance models, incorporating elements of the Bankes coat of arms and crest, the fleur-de-lis and moor's head. William's employment of Italian craftsmen to make things after a *mélange* of usually Renaissance models, often to a design made by himself, and frequently in some rare or particularly exquisite stone or marble selected by him, is one of the most striking and individual aspects of his patronage.

William also collaborated – and it was much more of a collaboration than his effective dictation to his purely Italian craftsmen in Italy – with Carlo Marochetti over the shrine of his ancestors in the Loggia, which was to be his major sculptural project right up to the end of his life. Marochetti seems to have met William in Paris around 1838. Their first scheme was to have included Chief Justice Bankes, Dame Mary and Charles I, but in the form of busts, not whole-length statues. Once in exile, William's schemes became more ambitious. In October 1844, in a letter to his brother George, he for the first time mentions the Loggia at Kingston Lacy as the locus of the intended sculpture. He also refers to his surviving drawing for a full-length statue of Brave Dame Mary. In it she holds the keys of Corfe Castle in one hand and a sword in the other, and stands in a niche, on a base decorated with a coat of arms, and flanked by two trophy-hung 'candelabra'. Barring the omitted candelabra, this was very much the scheme as finally executed.

A letter of 17 October 1853 from Marochetti makes it clear that the project of the Bankes pantheon had been revived. There were now to be three statues, three pedestals with reliefs, and accessories (in the form of four 'candelabra' – two in the form of cannon on their butt-ends, flanking Dame Mary, and two in the form of torches, flanking the Chief Justice), all in bronze. The contract, for £2,500, was signed in November 1853, and was to be performed within two years. Standing statues of Chief Justice Sir John Bankes and Dame Mary were to be associated with a seated statue of Charles I.

When William died, the two statues of the Chief Justice and Dame Mary were ready for casting, as was the relief of the siege of Corfe Castle, which was designed to go under the King, thus tying their loyalty in to the cause of their monarch. The statue of Charles I had been begun, but evidently none of the candelabra or their accessories. William's heirs must have taken account of what money had already been advanced to Marochetti, and have got him to agree to complete and cast all three statues and their reliefs, but to omit the candelabra.

With Walter Bankes, the story of collecting at Kingston Lacy comes to a virtual stop; indeed he was responsible for the one significant disposal from Kingston Lacy, of Velázquez's whole-length portrait of *Philip IV of Spain* from the Spanish Room in 1896 to Isabella Stewart Gardner. A little of the £10,000 he received was used to buy a second Zurbaran shop-work whole-length, of *St Elizabeth of Portugal* (No. 94) to fill the gap left on the wall. It seems likely that a rather better purchase, of the four *Elements* (Nos 43, 44, 46, 47) by Jan Brueghel the Younger and Hendrick van Balen, was made later.

After this, there are just two further losses to record: of the (since recovered) *Study of the head of Edward Altham* (for No. 70), after 1905; and the *Head of the poet Quevedo*, more probably after than by Velázquez, which the *marchand-amateur* Paul Wallraf bought from Ralph Bankes in 1938, and sold to the Spanish art historian Xavier de Salas. The former resurfaced in America and was bought back for Kingston Lacy in 1995, to make the extraordinary survival of the first Ralph Bankes's collection yet more complete.

The Loggia, with Marochetti's sculptures of Brave Dame Mary and Charles I

CHAPTER EIGHT
TOUR OF THE HOUSE

THE ENTRANCE HALL

William Bankes formed a new Entrance Hall at basement level by lowering the ground eight feet on the north side of the house and added the *porte-cochère* to Barry's design in the 1830s. The Hall, though rather low and dark, is dignified by Doric columns and a compartmented ceiling enlivened by egg-and-dart moulding and guilloche ornament. Bankes saw this kind of sub-hall when he visited Amesbury Abbey in Wiltshire, another house thought at the time to be by Inigo Jones.

SCULPTURE

ON LEFT:

Attributed to ALESSANDRO ALGARDI (1598–1654)
An unknown Roman (called Sir John Bankes)
Marble
Set up·here (and acquired?) only in 1913.

ON LEFT AND RIGHT:

Pair of 'oriental red granite' tables, with white marble scrolled supports on paw feet, the sides carved with shells, fruit, a lizard and a moth. Ordered by Bankes in Italy, and probably those carved by Salesio Pegrassi of Verona and described in 1849.

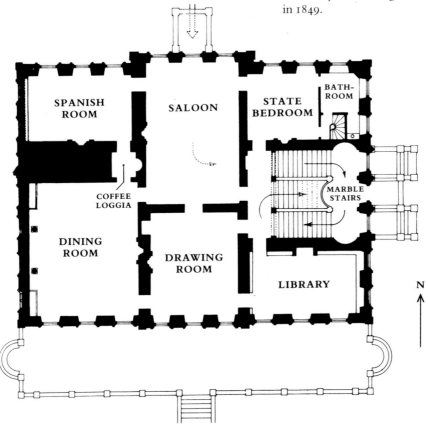

The Entrance Hall

FURNITURE

ON LEFT:

Late seventeenth-century Flemish ebony cabinet on stand. The doors are inset with reliefs imitating bronze of Venus and Cupid.

ON RIGHT:

Charles II lacquer cabinet on giltwood stand.

Six ebony chairs, bought by William Bankes from Emanuel Brothers of Bishopsgate *c.*1838.

CERAMICS

IN WINDOWS:

Pair of composition basket jardinières by Pegrassi shipped from Venice in 1846.

ON TABLES:

Two terracotta jardinières, modelled on two bronze well-heads by Niccolò dei Conti and Alfonso Alberghetti of 1556 and 1559 in the courtyard of the Doge's Palace in Venice. Commissioned from Angelo Giordani in July 1848 for 'twelve gold Napoleons'.

ON CABINETS:

Pair of K'ang Hsi blue-and-white jars and covers with formal lotus decoration.

METALWORK

BELOW BUST:

Collection of eighteenth- and nineteenth-century French and Venetian bronze door furniture, some cast by Giordani.

Pair of large nineteenth-century Japanese bronze cranes.

THE INNER HALL

SCULPTURE

Chimneypiece, carved with irises, lilies and William Bankes's coat of arms quartered with those of Wynne and Brune, and the family motto *Velle Quod Vult Deus* ('Desire what God wishes').

'Two openwork stoves in Carrara marble', commissioned from Pietro Lorandini in June 1850. Inscribed 'ΑΡΙΣΤΟΝ ΜΕΝ 'ΥΔΩΡ ('Water is best'). Their centres are inset with bronze medallions ordered from Baron Carlo Marochetti (1805–67) in October 1853 and based on Jean Goujon's medallion over the entrance to the Hôtel Carnavalet in Paris. That on the right shows Kingston Hall in its original state, and Pratt's plan for the main floor.

FLANKING CHIMNEYPIECE:

Pair of torchères, carved from Biancone marble from Bassano, probably by Pegrassi, one with fir and holly and the other with holly and ivy and birds.

METALWORK

IN FIREPLACE:

Pair of Paduan bronze andirons, surmounted by female figures attributed to Francesco Segala (1564–92). The tripod stands with rams' heads and grotesque winged masks do not belong to the figures and may be later. Originally intended by William Bankes for the Spanish Room.

ON STOVES:

Pair of oval brass urns, or *tazze*, nineteenth-century French Renaissance Revival. They are cast in relief with captives, winged masks and serpent handles.

THE MARBLE STAIRCASE

Barry created these Carrara marble stairs in the 1830s to provide William Bankes with a grand staircase worthy of a Roman *palazzo*, ascending to the state rooms on the first floor, or *piano nobile*, and above. The perspective is exaggerated by the descent of the ceiling vault against the ascent of the staircase to the Loggia on the half-landing. Bankes admired the staircase in the Palazzo Ruspoli in Rome, but the idea of the Loggia was Barry's.

THE LOGGIA

The first flight arrives on a half-landing at the airy loggia and garden entrance on the east, which look out into the park over the Dutch Garden, laid out at the turn of the century. The cedars beyond were planted by Bankes in 1835 as part of a projected 'green drive' to Pamphill village.

Barry proposed glazing bars for the windows and the plate glass does not seem to have been installed until 1849.

SCULPTURE

IN SHELL NICHES:

Baron CARLO MAROCHETTI (1805–67)
Bankes had been planning to commission these three monumental bronze figures of his famous ancestors and their king from Marochetti since the early 1840s, but he signed the contract in Paris only on 18 November 1853; the price was £2,500. The idea for the group seems to have come from another commemorating an event of the 1640s, Simon Guillain's *Louis XIII confiding the Regency of Louis XIV to Anne of Austria* (now in the Louvre). The bronze pedestals, which conceal radiators, are based on Verrocchio's tomb of Piero and Giovanni de' Medici in Florence. William died in 1855 without ever seeing the finished statues in place, and the pairs of candelabra he intended should flank the figures were never completed.

Sir John Bankes (1589–1644)
Attorney-General and Chief Justice of the Common Pleas to Charles I. Based on Gilbert Jackson's portrait (No. 9; Library).

Lady Bankes (1598–1661)
'Brave Dame Mary' holds her sword and the key of Corfe Castle, which she stoutly defended against the

Parliamentary besiegers. The head is based on Bone's enamel (in the Drawing Room) and the original miniature, the costume on Guillain's *Anne of Austria*.

Charles I (1600–49)
The bronze relief below showing the siege of Corfe Castle is based on a drawing by William Bankes.

Another two pairs of brass urns with masks, one with snakes for handles, the other with fruit, similar to those in the Inner Hall.

THE FIRST-FLOOR LANDING

The second flight reaches the *piano nobile* at a landing with three domes and five doorways of finely carved Biancone marble, three of them pedimented, which were supplied by Michelangelo Montresor in 1846. The doors lead, from the left, into the Library, the Drawing Room, the Saloon and the State Bedroom.

The last door but one was filled with a slab of grey marble on which is recorded the building history of the house, Inigo Jones being credited as the original architect because the family had long forgotten Sir Roger Pratt's involvement.

SCULPTURE

FLANKING SALOON DOORS:

Pair of Biancone marble candelabra, designed by Bankes, carved by Salesio Pegrassi and described in 1849. One is wreathed with olive and the other with myrtle, sacred to Minerva, the goddess of learning, and to Venus, the goddess of love, respectively. The medallion of Minerva was taken from an impression of a gem by Nathaniel Marchant in the Library sent over to Bankes in Italy.

OPPOSITE:

Two tapering bird figures, probably also by Pegrassi and shipped to Kingston Lacy in April 1854.

OVER STATE BEDROOM DOORCASE:

Nineteenth-century marble bust of Marcus Agrippa (63–12BC).

OVER LIBRARY DOORCASE:

Antique marble bust of Augustus (63BC–AD14), purchased in 1828 and mounted to match that of

his lifelong friend and supporter, Agrippa, in 1847. Augustus's proud boast – *lateritiam accepi marmoream reliqui* ('I found [Rome] brick and left it marble') – was no doubt chosen by Bankes to dignify his rebuilding of the house.

FURNITURE

Seventeenth-century French marquetry commode, possibly that purchased from Nixon & Son of Great Portland Street in February 1838.

THE LIBRARY

The Library was originally divided into a withdrawing room and Sir Ralph Bankes's closet. In its present form the room, with its bookcases, dates from the time of William Bankes's father, Henry Bankes (1757–1834), who employed the architect Robert Furze Brettingham (*c*.1750–1820, grandson of Matthew Brettingham senior), whom he met on his second visit to Rome in 1782, to make extensive alterations to the house on his return.

The Library was one of the last rooms William Bankes intended to transform, but his plans for raising and embellishing the ceiling were abandoned to please his sister, Lady Falmouth, who spent much time at Kingston Lacy after she was widowed in 1841.

PICTURES

FROM OVER ENTRANCE DOOR, CLOCKWISE:

1 Sir PETER LELY (1618–80)
? *Arabella Bankes, Mrs Gilly* (b.1642)
Sixth daughter of Sir John Bankes, and wife of Samuel Gilly of High Hall, Wimborne. Long thought to be of her sister Mary (see No. 5), but early on their identities became confused. Painted around the time that her brother Ralph built Kingston Lacy, and not only the loveliest portrait that he commissioned from Lely or acquired subsequently, but 'unsurpassed in Lely's career' (Sir Oliver Millar).

2 Sir PETER LELY (1618–80)
'*Mr Stafford*'
Almost certainly Edmund Stafford of Buckinghamshire; originally perhaps a friend of John Bankes, but later an Oxford contemporary and friend of Ralph, who would appear to have commissioned this portrait of him.

?Arabella Bankes, Mrs Gilly (b.1642); by Sir Peter Lely (No. 1; Library)

3 MASSIMO STANZIONE (?1585–?1656)
Jerome Bankes (1635/6–86)
Third son of Sir John Bankes. Probably painted in Naples, around 1655, when the sitter was on his Grand Tour. Stanzione was known for subject pictures, but it is typical of a travelling Englishman to have employed him for a portrait instead.

4 Sir PETER LELY (1618–80)
Elizabeth Trentham, Viscountess Cullen (1640–1713)
First recorded in 1731 simply as 'Lady Cullen', this portrait later came to be identified with the fifth daughter of Sir John Bankes, Jane, who actually died unmarried. The real sitter – no relation of the Bankeses – was notorious for her beauty, extravagance and immorality.

5 ? Studio of Sir PETER LELY (1618–80)
? Mary Bankes, Lady Jenkinson (1623–91)
Second daughter of Sir John Bankes, married in 1653 to Sir Robert Jenkinson, 1st Bt, of Walcot and Hawkesbury. Previously identified as a portrait of *Arabella Bankes, Mrs Gilly* (see No. 1), but this picture is too early to be of her, and may not even be by Lely.

6 Attributed to GERARD SEGHERS (1591–1651)
St Jerome (c.342–420)
One of a set of the Four Fathers of the Latin Church (see Nos 8, 15, 17). Seen producing his translation of the Bible into Latin (known as 'The Vulgate') with the help of angels, and identified (anachronistically) by his cardinal's hat.

7 Sir PETER LELY (1618–80)
Sir Ralph Bankes, MP (?1631–77)
Second, but eldest surviving, son of Sir John Bankes. Knighted 1660; builder of Kingston Lacy 1663–5 to Sir Roger Pratt's designs; and founder of the picture collection. Painted in the later 1650s. A later variant is at Yale.

8 Attributed to GERARD SEGHERS (1591–1651)
St Gregory the Great (c.540–604)
Shown composing his Moral Homilies with inspiration from the Holy Ghost in the form of a dove. Elected Pope, 590; sent St Augustine of Canterbury to convert the English in 596. See No. 6.

9 GILBERT JACKSON (active 1622–43)
Chief Justice Sir John Bankes, MP, PC (1589–1644)
Inscribed with his age (54) and the date (1643). Attorney-General and knighted 1634; Chief Justice of the Common Pleas, 1640/1; purchased the Kingston Lacy estate in 1632–6, and Corfe in 1635. The three-quarter-length portrait in the National Portrait Gallery was presented by W. R. Bankes.

10 RICHARD ROPER (active c.1735–c.1775)
John Bankes the Younger, MP (1692–1772)
Signed and dated 1764 on the back
Unmarried. Tory MP for Corfe Castle from 1722 to 1741, when he stood down in favour of his younger brother and heir Henry. John Bankes's choice of such an undistinguished painter – primarily a sporting artist – was typical of his negligence. Evidently done from the same sitting as No. 109 and as a pendant to the portrait of his brother (No. 110).

11 DUTCH, mid-seventeenth-century
A shipping scene
First listed in 1731 as 'A Sea Peice' by 'Vanderveld', paired with the Porcellis (No. 14), which had already been similarly over-attributed.

12 GILBERT JACKSON (active 1622–43)
Dr John Bankes (b.1569)
Signed *Gil. Jac. Fecit* and dated 1643
Father of Sir John Bankes, as a Doctor of Divinity, at the age of 74.

13 POMPEO BATONI (1708–87)
Henry Bankes the Younger, MP (1757–1834)
Signed: *POMPEO BATONI/PINX. ROM. 1779*
Painted on the Grand Tour, for the sitter's mother. Henry Bankes himself wrote to her that it was: 'a melancholy cold picture, whose only merit is being simple and having nothing offensive'. He preferred Reynolds.

Employed R. F. Brettingham to alter Kingston Lacy in the 1780s.

14 ?JULIUS PORCELLIS, known as PORCELLIS THE YOUNGER (*c.*1609–45)
Shipping in a rough sea
Panel
More probably by Julius than by his father Jan Porcellis (1587–1632), but, like No. 11, first recorded as by 'old Vanderveld' in 1731 and 1762.

15 Attributed to GERARD SEGHERS (1591–1651)
St Ambrose (*c.*334 or 340–397)
Writing DE FIDE AD GRATIANUM AUGUSTUM. Acclaimed Bishop of Milan, 374; baptised St Augustine, 387. See No. 6.

16 Sir PETER LELY (1618—80)
Charles Brune of Athelhampton (1630/1–?1703)
His niece Mary married Sir Ralph Bankes in 1661. This superb portrait will have been painted then or not long afterwards.

17 Attributed to GERARD SEGHERS (1591–1651)
St Augustine of Hippo (354–430)
Seen writing *The City of God*, having been discouraged from plumbing the mystery of the Trinity by the child, who flourishes a wooden spoon, to indicate that he had as much chance of emptying the ocean with that. Bishop of Hippo from *c.*396.

The Library

BOOKS

This is very much a family library, reflecting the interests of several generations of the Bankes family. They bought both English and foreign publications and appear to have been mainly interested in history, politics, literature and travel. The changing shape of the collection can be traced through the seventeenth-century inventory and its supplements, and the inventories of 1856, 1860 and 1905.

The core of the library was assembled during the Civil War. Little remains of Sir John Bankes's library from Corfe Castle, which was granted to Cromwell's Sergeant, Sir John Maynard, by Parliament in October 1645. The only survivors may be two books formerly owned by Sir Nicholas Bacon, one of which has an elaborate armorial binding by Jean de Planche. Sir John's sons, who travelled on the Continent for their education during the Commonwealth, were enthusiastic book collectors. John frequently signed his acquisitions in France and Italy, often also noting the prices he paid. Ralph lists and comments in French or Latin upon his reading in his commonplace books, dated ?1656–9, 1657 and 1666. He may also have collected the seventeenth-century volumes of architectural engravings.

Henry Bankes the Elder marked many of his purchases with a bookplate, whilst others signed theirs: Margaret Bankes (née Parker), John Wynne, Frances Woodley and William John Bankes, to name but a few. Nine of the expensive folio volumes of the *Description de l'Egypte* (1809–28) were bought in Paris in July 1818. The library also contains two editions of Ratti's Genoa guides (1766, 1780), in which William comments on the two Rubenses he purchased there (Nos 57 and 59), as well as the picaresque *Life and Adventures of Giovanni Finati* (1830), his travelling companion in the Middle East, which he edited (see Chapter Four). Unfortunately, William never published an account of his own travels in the East, although the lithographic stones intended to be used for the plates have survived.

An armorial binding by Jean de Planche, one of only two books thought to have survived here from Sir John Bankes's library at Corfe Castle

SCULPTURE

Baron CARLO MAROCHETTI (1805–67)
Carlo Botta (1767–1837)
Doctor and historian of his native Piedmont, Italy, and the United States, Botta began as a campaigner for an independent republic of Italy, and ended as an academic in France. The sculptor would appear to have given William Bankes this bronze as supporting evidence of his suitability to execute the monument to Wellington in Glasgow (1841–4).

FURNITURE

OVER CHIMNEYPIECE:

The keys of Corfe Castle, which Lady Bankes was allowed to retain as a mark of her courage, with a spur and cannonballs from the siege.

'One hundred impressions of gems', engraved from antique statues in Rome by Nathaniel Marchant (1739–1816) and acquired by Henry Bankes.

Regency rosewood writing-table with brass edges and fluted splayed feet, in the manner of John

McClean & Son, the London firm of cabinetmakers active in the early nineteenth century.

Pair of Regency terrestrial and celestial library globes, made by Smith's.

CARPET

Axminster, with 'a Persian design', bought by Henry Bankes from Samuel Whitty on 12 October 1819 for £60 16s.

THE DRAWING ROOM

Sir Ralph Bankes's great parlour of the 1660s became the Drawing Room in the 1780s and Henry Bankes's chimneypiece and doors survive from this time, the latter moved by William from the adjacent bedroom. Barry raised the ceiling in the 1830s, basing the design on a ceiling at Lees Court, Kent, another 'Inigo Jones' house visited by William Bankes (destroyed by fire in 1910). The stencil for the Bankes motto *Velle Quod Vult Deus* along the frieze was sent from Venice in 1846.

The room was largely refurnished by the late Mr Bankes's mother, Henrietta, and it retains the character of a cluttered Edwardian drawing-room. She re-covered the walls in rose damask the year after her marriage to Walter Ralph Bankes in 1897, and covered the sofa and chairs in green striped silk, both from Haynes of Spring Street, Paddington. Photographs of her can be seen on the piano and the desk.

SCULPTURE

The surround for the double doors to the Saloon cost 1,000 Austrian lire in July 1846. The four door architraves of the yellow marble of Torre were executed in Verona by Michelangelo Montresor in the same year, as were those in the Dining Room and Saloon.

FLANKING DOORS TO SALOON:

Pair of console tables, carved in pale Sienna marble, with green marble medallions. The lions' heads were drawn by Bankes and based on designs by the Florentine Renaissance sculptor Bartolomeo Ammanati (1511–92). The tables were made by Antonio Ferrari in Rome, who estimated for the marble at 170 scudi and making them at 540 scudi in 75 days in October 1844.

PICTURES

FROM OVER DOOR TO DINING ROOM, CLOCKWISE:

18 ENGLISH, ?1650s
? Sir Henry Parker, 2nd Bt, of Honington
(c.1640–1713)
Cf. No. 112. The identification is traditional, but the picture may actually be of the 1680s.

19 HENRY WEIGALL Jr (?1829–1925)
Rose Louise Bastard, Mrs Bankes
Monogrammed and dated 1865
Daughter of Percival Bastard of Stourpaine, married Edmund George Bankes in 1848.

20 HENRY BONE, RA (1755–1834) after PAOLO VERONESE (1528–88)
Venus and Cupid
Enamel on copper
The original painting (not unanimously accepted as by Veronese) was acquired from the Colonna collection in Rome by the banker-collector J. Sloane, but belonged to Sir Simon Clarke, Bt, when Bone made this enamel of it.

21 MARY GOW, Mrs SYDNEY PRIOR HALL (1851–1929)
Henrietta Jenny Fraser, Mrs Bankes (d.1953) *with her elder daughter Daphne* (b.1898)
Watercolour, dated 1902
Daughter of William Thompson Fraser, married Walter Ralph Bankes in 1897.

22 Sir JOSHUA REYNOLDS, PRA (1723–92)
Frances Payne, Mrs Woodley (1738–1813)
Oval
Only daughter of Abraham Payne, of the Leeward Islands, married in 1758 to William Woodley. Mother of Frances, Mrs Henry Bankes the Younger. Painted as a marriage portrait, 1758–60. Also shown in the Zoffany upstairs (No. 118).

23 Sir THOMAS LAWRENCE, PRA (1769–1830)
Anne Frances Bankes, Lady Falmouth (1789–1864)
Sister of William Bankes, married in 1810 to Edward Boscawen, 4th Viscount and 1st Earl of Falmouth (d.1841). Stayed at Kingston Lacy as a widow. Thought to have been painted as a marriage portrait.

24 Sir ANTHONY VAN DYCK (1599–1641)
Sir John Borlase, 1st Bt, MP (1619–72)
Scion of a Cornish family settled in Buckinghamshire, Borlase was a slightly reluctant Royalist, though imprisoned after Penruddock's rising in

The Drawing Room

1655. MP for Corfe Castle, 1641–4, and for Chipping [High] Wycombe, 1661–72. Created baronet 1642. A copy of this picture is at Sudbury Hall.

25 Sir ANTHONY VAN DYCK (1599–1641)
Alice Bankes, Lady Borlase (1621–83)
Eldest daughter of Sir John Bankes, married (Sir) John Borlase (No. 24) in 1637. Converted to Catholicism after taking the waters at Bourbon in her widowhood, and died in Paris, where she had done good works amongst the poor.

26 GEORGE DOWDNEY (active 1730s)
John Bankes the Younger, MP (1692–1772)
Inscribed and dated 1733 on obverse
The obscure artist had previously restored most of the pictures in the collection, in 1731. See No. 10 (Library) for the sitter.

27 ENGLISH, *c.*1630
Ralph Hawtrey of Ruislip (1570–1638)
Father of Lady Bankes.

28 Sir THOMAS LAWRENCE, PRA (1769–1830)
Maria Woodley, Mrs Riddell (1772–1808)
Sister of Frances Woodley, married Lt Walter Riddell in 1790. An author and poet, whose admirers included Robert Burns (who addressed flattering and satirical poems to her). Exh. RA, 1806.

29 GEORGE ROMNEY (1734–1802)
Frances Woodley, Mrs Bankes (1760–1823)
Eldest daughter of William Woodley (cf. No. 118),
married Henry Bankes the Younger in 1784. A
celebrated beauty. Mother of William Bankes, on
whom she doted. Painted 1780–1.

30 Sir THOMAS LAWRENCE, PRA (1769–1830)
Charlotte Dee, Lady Nugent (1756–1813)
Painted in 1789 as Mrs Johnstone, for the Marquis
of Abercorn. Later wife of Admiral Sir Charles
Nugent and mistress of the Duke of Cumberland,
who fathered the daughter (No. 87) who married
George Bankes. Unfinished.

31 ENGLISH, c.1630
Mary Altham, Mrs Hawtrey (1578–1647)
Daughter of Edward Altham the Elder (d.1605) and
Elizabeth Barne (d.1621). Aunt of Edward Altham
the hermit (No. 70). Wife of Ralph Hawtrey, and
mother of Lady Bankes.

32 GEORGE DOWDNEY (active 1730s)
Henry Bankes the Elder, MP (1698–1776)
Dated 1734 on reverse
For the sitter, see No. 110.

MINIATURES

BELOW PAINTINGS:

Here hangs the greater part of a collection of 50
enamel miniatures painted on copper by Henry
Bone, RA (1755–1834), the greatest British artist
ever to practise in this demanding medium, and
another five by his son, Henry Pierce Bone (1779–
1855). They mostly portray Queen Elizabeth I and
her courtiers and contemporaries, but include two
of Brave Dame Mary, by father and son, both after a
miniature (now gone) by John Hoskins (active
c.1620–d.1664/5). William Bankes acquired the
enamels at auction in 1836, from a set of 85 which
had been unsuccessfully offered to the nation for

Part of William Bankes's collection of enamel portrait miniatures by Henry Bone above a Sienna marble console table in the Drawing Room

£4,000 by the elder Bone. William gave the bulk of them to his brother, the Rev. Edward Bankes, but after his flight abroad in 1841, Edward had a fit of conscience and returned them to Kingston Lacy, where they have traditionally hung in a serried rank in the Drawing Room ever since.

FURNITURE

Three large seventeenth-century scrolled crestings, with the cipher 'WJB', like those in the Dining Room. They were plausibly called 'Bavarian' by William Bankes.

French nineteenth-century *secrétaire à abattant* with a porcelain plaque, which was in the Saloon in 1856.

Carlton House desk, inlaid with marquetry of flower swags and gardening trophies. The slots in the top take letters.

Blackamoors balancing flower tubs on their feet.

The screen and piano stool on lyre supports, covered in painted velvet, came from Henrietta Bankes's London house.

CERAMICS

ON CONSOLE TABLES:

Blue-and-white fan-shaped Delftware flower-holders, one with a portrait bust of William III, possibly acquired by John Bankes the Elder in the 1690s.

LEFT OF FIREPLACE:

Famille rose bowl painted with a British East Indiaman.

Nineteenth-century Meissen groups and figures, which are among the china collected by Henrietta Bankes.

CARPET

Savonnerie of about 1830, with central medallion on a pink ground and scrolling foliate border.

THE DINING ROOM

In Pratt's house, this was the south-west apartment, one of four suites placed at the corners of the house, which here consisted of a square, wainscoted room and two closets (one originally containing a small set of back stairs). The apartment still survived in

1791, when it was being used by Henry and Frances Bankes as their bedroom and dressing-rooms.

By the early nineteenth century the family needed a larger dining-room for entertaining. Various schemes were proposed for enlarging the eating room in the north-west corner of the house (now the Spanish Room) before Barry created the present room in the 1830s by removing the internal partitions and north wall, and taking in Brettingham's adjoining family staircase.

Later in the nineteenth century William's still unfinished decorative scheme seems to have been damaged by fire, and only the highly carved 'Bavarian' crestings above the windows, the walnut shutters carved from his own designs, the ceiling and the boxwood doors (see below) survive. After the fire Walter Ralph Bankes panelled the room in oak and cedar wood grown in the park.

CEILING

Barry's ceiling was inspired by those at another Pratt house, Coleshill in Berkshire (destroyed by fire in 1952).

DOORS

The panels for the four pairs of double doors were carved in boxwood by Vincenzo Favenza in Venice between 1849 and 1853. The subjects are taken from Donatello's High Altar in the Santo of Padua.

ORGAN

The organ was installed here in the 1880s, having perhaps been moved from the Saloon where it was designed to go above the large doors into the Drawing Room and played from a console within the Drawing Room cupboard doors.

PICTURES

33 SEBASTIANO DEL PIOMBO (c.1485–1547)
The Judgement of Solomon
According to I *Kings*, iii, 16–28, two harlots who had had babies were disputing whose was the one who had not died. Solomon (in the centre) showed his wisdom by threatening to have his executioner (on the extreme right) divide it equally between them. The real mother (on the right) immediately revealed herself by offering to give up her claim in favour of the false mother (on the left), in order to save her baby's life.

This is a flawed masterpiece of the Venetian High

The Judgement of Solomon; by Sebastiano del Piombo, c.1505–10 (No.33; Dining Room)

Renaissance, painted around 1505–10, and was neither finished nor resolved: recent restoration has revealed three different conceptions of figures and settings overlaying one another. The judicial subject may originally have been commissioned for one of the courtrooms in the Doge's Palace in Venice by Andrea Loredan, builder of the Palazzo di San Marcuola, subsequently known as the Casa Grimani de Santo Ermacora (now the Palazzo Vendramin-Calergi), where it seems first to have been recorded by Ridolfi in 1648. He attributed that picture to Giorgione, and this was bought as such by William Bankes in 1820 from the Marescalchi collection in Bologna. In 1903 Berenson attributed it to Sebastiano, who is now generally accepted as its author.

34 Mrs ANN HOWARD (? née BROWN) after MICHAEL DAHL (1656/9–1743)
James Butler, 2nd Duke of Ormonde (1665–1745)
After the painting in the National Portrait Gallery dated 1714. Mrs Howard, the copyist named in the 1762 catalogue, is not otherwise recorded; it is possible that she is the same as the Ann Brown, active from 1698 to 1720, by whom there were copies at Ickworth in Suffolk and Dalkeith in Midlothian.

The sitter's grandfather, the 1st Duke of Ormonde, leased Kingston Lacy and died in the house in 1688.

35 After Sir PETER LELY (1618–80)
Edward Hyde, 1st Earl of Clarendon (1609–74)
Lord Chancellor, historian of the Civil War, and father-in-law of James II. Cousin of Margaret Hyde, Lady Parker (cf. No. 116) – but this portrait of him was only a later acquisition. The original whole-length version is at Chequers.

36 After Sir ANTHONY VAN DYCK (1599–1641)
The Betrayal of Christ
First recorded in the collection in 1731, as by Rubens, but actually a copy of the picture in the Prado.

? Nicolò Zen; by Titian, 1540s (No. 45; Dining Room)

45 TITIAN (*c.*1488/90–1565)
? Nicolò Zen (1515–65)

Inscribed on the back of the canvas: *CA ZORZI*
Bought by William Bankes in Bologna in 1820, from the Marescalchi collection, as an unknown senator of the Savorgnan family, its previous owners; but the recent discovery of an early copy of the head, inscribed 'Nicolò Zen', makes it highly probable that this is the lost portrait of '*M. Niccolò Zono*', mentioned by Vasari in 1567 as among Titian's later portraits. Stylistically, it would seem to date from the early 1560s. Nicolò Zen(o) was a *Savio di terraferma* and a Knight (either of which would account for the colour of his robe), a member of the Council of Ten, and had served as ambassador to Charles V in 1545. He was also an author, and a friend of the publisher Francesco Marcolini, and of such patrons of Titian as Pietro Aretino and Daniele Barbaro.

37 JACOPO PALMA, known as PALMA GIOVANE (*c.*1548–1628)
An Allegory of Prophecy

One of two pictures then attributed to 'Bonifacio', acquired by William Bankes in 1849 off the ceiling of the Palazzo Capello a San Felice in Venice and intended for the ceiling of the Library. Its message was identified by an old inscription as: *Sapientiam antiquorum exquivet sapiens et in prophetis vacabit* ('The wise man seeks out the wisdom of the Ancients, and has leisure for the prophets'). The wisdom of the Ancients appears to be exemplified by the philosopher-king Numa (here given a fleur-de-lisé crown, possibly emblematic of Henri III, who returned via Venice from the throne of Poland to that of France in 1574), presiding over the Augurs, who foretell the future from the flight of birds.

38 ALONSO CANO (1601–67) and Studio
The Coronation of the Virgin

Bought by William Bankes in Spain in 1814; one of only two survivors (the other is No. 92) of the 'many of Alonso Cano, which I have brought from Convents in Granada & the interior'. Cano probably originated this much-repeated composition after retiring to Granada in 1652.

39 ? BOLOGNESE, seventeenth-century

Four painted hangings bought from a Palazzo Cambiaso in Genoa, by William Bankes, as by Annibale Carracci. Regarded by him as the finest of all his acquisitions.

(a) *Prometheus stealing fire from the chariot of the sun*
(b) *Hercules and Antaeus*
(c) *The Rape of Ganymede*
(d) *Neptune and Theophane*

SCULPTURE

ON CHIMNEYPIECE:

After HUBERT LE SUEUR (*c.*1585–1658)
Charles I (1600–49), 1839
Bronze

Cast in Paris by Forbier for William Bankes, evidently before he had conceived the idea of a family shrine of full-length figures centring on the King in the Loggia.

Two Torre yellow marble vases carved with lion skins, bearded masks and vine leaves, carved by Barrini in June 1853 for 500 Austrian lire.

FURNITURE

BELOW *JUDGEMENT OF SOLOMON*:

Late sixteenth-century Italian poker-work coffer in cedarwood. The cartouche on the top is inscribed 'Barbarus Hyde'.

BELOW *NICOLÒ ZEN*:

Dutch table in the style of Daniel Marot, possibly that bought from John Webb of 8 Old Bond Street in 1839 for £20 as 'a very fine Venetian table'.

BELOW VERDURE TAPESTRY:

'A large mahogany semi oval sideboard curiously inlaid with various different colour'd woods', bought by Henry Bankes from Ince & Mayhew on 30 August 1786 for £29 18s 3d.

Two stained limewood pendant appliqués, richly carved in the style of Grinling Gibbons with game, fruit and foliage.

FLANKING CHIMNEYPIECE:

Two early seventeenth-century Roman carved walnut *cassoni*, or marriage chests, acquired by William Bankes in Italy, one carved with Neptune, Amphitrite and merfolk, the other with Orpheus and the animals.

Mahogany dining-table with expanding segmental panels.

Set of eighteen William IV mahogany dining-chairs covered in giraffe hide.

Victorian chandelier by F. & C. Osler of Birmingham, bought at the Milton Abbey sale in 1932.

TAPESTRY

Early eighteenth-century English verdure tapestry depicting Apollo and Daphne, probably woven in the Soho factory. Acquired by W. R. Bankes.

CARPET

Early nineteenth-century Savonnerie with central medallion on an olive green field and scrolling border with griffins and flower baskets.

THE COFFEE LOGGIA

This small room was created by Barry for William Bankes and is also accessible from the Spanish Room. It has a vaulted ceiling ingeniously lit by a lamp above the alabaster boss and two niches with shell heads. The Coffee Loggia shows Barry's flair as a designer and his skilful use of space behind the backstairs, from which light is borrowed through the alabaster niche and increased by mirror glass. The 'floor of inlaid woods' from Italy was laid in 1849.

SCULPTURE

Pair of console tables in Biancone marble by Michelangelo Montresor, sent from Verona to Venice in 1845.

THE SALOON

The ante-room, or double-height hall, of Pratt's original house had a large gallery or *pergolo* at the south end which made the hall itself into a cube. It was taken down early in the eighteenth century, when Pratt's cornice was extended round the south end.

The room became the Saloon or Ballroom early in the younger Henry Bankes's time, when, influenced perhaps by his Dorset neighbours at Milton Abbey and Bryanston, he employed the architect Robert Furze Brettingham on his return from Rome in 1782 to build the coved ceiling and the existing cornice and frieze. Henry Bankes also installed the white and gold curtain boxes over the windows. Their lion-headed shield medallions are echoed in the ceiling, which was probably painted by Cornelius Dixon in 1790. He is recorded as an 'ornament painter' at Strawberry Hill and Thomas Anson of Shugborough's town house, 15 St James's Square.

William Bankes, according to his notebooks for the years 1836–40, intended the Saloon walls to be hung with the late seventeenth-century Gobelins tapestries from the *Triomphes des Dieux* series he had previously acquired for his Welsh house, Soughton, together with the four 'Carraccis' painted on cloth. However, he decided to hang the walls with paintings, and so sent the tapestries to Soughton; the 'Carraccis' are now in the Dining Room (No. 39).

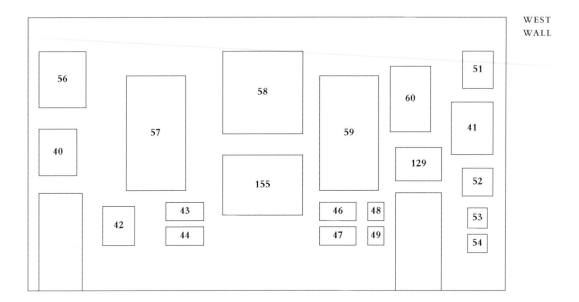

WEST
WALL

SCULPTURE

Marble chimneypiece by John Flaxman (1755–1826), who was paid £66 6s for chimneypieces in March 1786, the year before he went to Italy.

The niches were designed by Barry in 1840 following sketches made by William Bankes, which he based on shell niches in Montpellier and Narbonne. The shells were carved in yellow Torre marble by Michelangelo Montresor in Verona in November 1847, and the architraves are of Biancone. The backs of the niches were cut from purple and white *mischio di Seravezza* or *fleur de pêcher* marble by Seymour in 1854, following detailed instructions from William Bankes, given during a visit to Kingston Lacy towards the end of his life.

PICTURES

40 BENEDETTO GENNARI (1633–1715)
Lady Elizabeth Howard, Lady Felton (1656–81)
Portrayed as Cleopatra and painted for the Duke of Monmouth, around 1678/9. The sitter was wife of Sir Thomas Felton, 4th Bt, Comptroller of the Household to Charles II's queen, Catherine of Braganza, who particularly patronised the Catholic Gennari in England.

41 DUTCH CARAVAGGESQUE, second quarter of the seventeenth century
A man with a glass of wine and fiddle

Described as a 'Nightpeice of A man A drinking' in the very first list of Ralph Bankes's pictures, at Gray's Inn *c.*1656.

42 Circle of RAPHAEL (1485–1520)
The Holy Family with the Infant St John in a Landscape
Bought as a Raphael in Spain in 1813 by William Bankes (see p.40), who commissioned the frame carved with medallions of the supposed previous owners from Pietro Giusti in Siena in 1853. It has been reattributed to one of Raphael's late Roman pupils, Giulio Romano (1499–1546) or G. F. Penni (1488–1528), but it seems closer to an earlier period of Raphael's career in character.

On the back of the panel are the brands of two of its certain previous owners, Vincenzo I Gonzaga, 4th Duke of Mantua (1562–1612), and King Charles I, who bought the bulk of the Gonzaga collections in 1626–8. Acquired for Philip IV of Spain during the Commonwealth, it was looted by the French from the sacristy of the Escorial in the Peninsular War.

43 Attributed to JAN BRUEGHEL THE YOUNGER (1601–78) and HENDRICK VAN BALEN (1575–1632)
The Four Elements: Air
On copper
The set was bought after 1905. Although the compositions are derived from Jan Brueghel the

Elder's (1568–1625) set of *Elements* painted for Cardinal Federico Borromeo, Van Balen's figures here are not found in any of the innumerable copies and derivatives of these, and the quality of execution is superb. Air is personified by a figure of Astronomy.

44 Attributed to JAN BRUEGHEL THE YOUNGER (1601–78) and HENDRICK VAN BALEN (1575–1632)
The Four Elements: Water
On copper
Water is personified by a figure probably representing one of the Nymphs seduced by Neptune, who can be seen riding in triumph on the sea in the background.

46 Attributed to JAN BRUEGHEL THE YOUNGER (1601–78) and HENDRICK VAN BALEN (1575–1632)
The Four Elements: Earth
On copper
The personification of Earth appears to be a composite figure derived from such embodiments of the generative abundance of Nature as Cybele and Pomona. The two leopards occur in a number of works by Brueghel the Elder, but not in his original of this composition.

47 Attributed to JAN BRUEGHEL THE YOUNGER (1601–78) and HENDRICK VAN BALEN (1575–1632)
The Four Elements: Fire
On copper
The main protagonists here are the lovers Mars and Venus, with the forge of Vulcan, the latter's cuckolded husband, to the left.

48 After CARLO MARATTA (1625–1713)
The Virgin Annunciate
A late and inferior acquisition.

49 After GERRIT DOU (1613–75)
Lovers singing by candlelight
'A coppy' bought by Ralph Bankes before 1659 from Lely, who owned the original, which is now in the Royal Collection.

51 ENGLISH, *c.*1650–60
Portrait of an unknown scholar
Possibly by the same hand as a group of similar portraits at Chirk Castle in Clwyd. Its eighteenth-century Rococo frame is a pendant to that of Chief Justice Bankes (No. 9), but the sitter's identity had already been lost when it was made.

52 PEETER NEEFS THE ELDER (*c.*1578–1657/61)
The interior of an imaginary cathedral
Signed: *Peeter Neefs 164[4?]*
It is difficult to distinguish between father and son Neefs, both of whom repeatedly painted interiors of imaginary cathedrals more or less closely based on that of Antwerp, following the example set by Hendrick Steenwyck the Elder (*c.*1550–1603), such a picture by whom was in Ralph Bankes's collection.

53 GERMAN, *c.*1520–30
An unknown man
Belonged to Ralph Bankes in 1659, when thought to be: 'A Coppy after Holbein'.

54 DUTCH, seventeenth-century
Flowers hanging by a ribbon
First recorded at Kingston Lacy in 1731.

55 After GUIDO RENI (1585–1642)
The Adoration of the Shepherds
An adapted copy of the octagonal painting formerly at Houghton Hall in Norfolk, and now in the Pushkin Museum, Moscow. In one of the eighteenth-century imitations of Sunderland frames peculiar to Kingston Lacy.

56 After Sir ANTHONY VAN DYCK (1599–1641)
King Charles I (1600–49)
The face is derived from that of the standing portrait of the King in his robes of state at Windsor, but no original of this particular portrait type is known.

57 Sir PETER PAUL RUBENS (1577–1640)
? Marchesa Maria Serra Pallavicino
Signed on base of niche at left: PETRˢ. PAVLVS RVEB[EÑ]S/PINXIT AT[Q]UE/SINGVLARI DEVOTIÕE/D D/ M. DC. VI
One of the first, and the most beautiful, of the epoch-making portraits painted by Rubens on his visits to Genoa, this and No. 59 were acquired by William Bankes from that city in 1840, as of the *marchese* Isabella and Maria Grimaldi respectively. Those identities would appear, however, to have been conferred upon them by the Grimaldi family, which had latterly owned them. When first referred to, in Ratti's guide to Genoa of 1780, they were anonymous. New research into the heraldic motifs of the curtain drawn up above this sitter's head has identified her as Maria Serra, the wife of Niccolò Pallavicino, banker and host to Rubens's employer, Duke Vincenzo I Gonzaga of Mantua, whose hospitality in 1606 included a sumptuous banquet and ball, at which she probably wore the lavish

dress in which she is portrayed. Hence the fact that Rubens painted this portrait as a gift (*D[ono] D[edit]*) – no doubt by proxy for his master.

58 Sir PETER LELY (1618–80)
St Mary Magdalene
Painted *c*.1650–5, employing a model who occurs in a number of Lely's paintings and drawings of the period. Belonged to Ralph Bankes by about 1656.

59 Sir PETER PAUL RUBENS (1577–1640)
? Marchesa Maria Grimaldi and her dwarf
Inscribed on the dog's collar: M^y AM (?)
Acquired with No. 57, but not necessarily originally its pendant. In which case the facts that it was

? Marchesa Maria Grimaldi; by Sir Peter Paul Rubens (No. 59; Saloon)

recorded by Ratti in 1780 as hanging in the apartment of Giovanbattista Grimaldi la Pietra, and that the letters on the dog's collar may be a garbling of 'MARIA', could mean that the traditional identification of the sitter as the *marchesa* Maria Grimaldi is correct. It was her father, the *marchese* Carlo Grimaldi, who put his villa at Sampadierna at the disposal of Rubens and his employer, Duke Vincenzo I Gonzaga of Mantua, in 1607.

60 After Sir ANTHONY VAN DYCK (1599–1641)
Queen Henrietta Maria (1609–69)
This is one of a number of versions of a portrait of the Queen in blue (now lost), for which Van Dyck submitted an account to Charles I in 1638.

62 ? GEORGE GELDORP (*c*.1595–1665) after Sir ANTHONY VAN DYCK (1599–1641)
The head of Jacomo de Cachiopin (1575–1642)
Sold as an unfinished original to Ralph Bankes by George Geldorp, but in fact copied from a three-quarter-length portrait now in the Kunsthistorisches Museum, Vienna; Geldorp was a notorious copyist and pasticheur of Van Dyck. Cachiopin was a passionate collector of pictures by Van Dyck, devoting a whole room of his country house to them.

63 ? N. WRAY (active *c*.1650–60) after CLAUDE MELLAN (1598–1688)
The Madonna
Described in 1659 as: 'A Madonna, Coppied in Rome from A Print of Milan. N. Wray. £12.' Wray is here listed as the vendor, but it seems unlikely that he would have known such a circumstantial detail about *where* a print had been copied unless he had also been the copyist.

64 After REMBRANDT (1606–69)
An Oriental
Listed by Ralph Bankes in 1659 as: 'A Coppy of A Turks head from Rainebrand. The orriginall is Cardinall Mazarins sister[s] ... £20 – his top valuation bar four. The flecks on the man's face are not just discolourations of the paint, but are thought to represent leprosy: it might therefore represent the opulent Naaman, whom Elisha healed of his leprosy. The original is at Chatsworth.

65 After FEDERICO BAROCCIO (?1535–1612)
St Michelina of Pesaro (?1300–56)
Derived from the original full-length in the Vatican. St Michelina was a Franciscan tertiary known for good works.

EAST
WALL

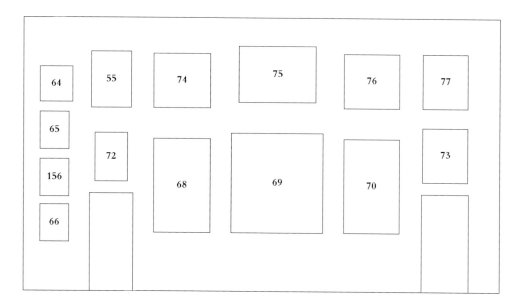

66 JORIS VAN SON (1623–67)
Fruit and corn hanging by a ribbon
Signed and dated 1654
Belonged to Ralph Bankes in 1659.

68 Studio of Sir ANTHONY VAN DYCK
(1599–1641)
Sir Richard Weston, 1st Earl of Portland, KG
(1577–1634/5)
Chancellor of the Exchequer, 1620/1–8 and Lord
High Treasurer, 1628–35. He enjoyed the confidence of Charles I, but was unpopular with the
country, as a crypto-Catholic who favoured peace
with Spain, in order that the King could live off his
own, without having to summon Parliament to
raise taxes. The original of this portrait, showing
him as Lord High Treasurer, is lost.

69 NICOLAES BERCHEM (1620–83)
Landscape with herdsmen
Signed and dated 1655
Recorded as either commissioned from the artist in
Haarlem, or bought, through Sir Peter Lely by
Ralph Bankes for £32, including its (previous)
frame, and first listed in his collection at Gray's Inn
in *c*.1658. It is an exceptional size for this artist,
making it more likely to have been a specific
commission.

70 EDWARD ALTHAM (1629–94)
Self-portrait as a hermit
A cousin of Jerome Bankes, with whom he was in
Italy. Painted in Rome, where he had arrived by
1650, was received into the Church in 1652, and
lived until his death. Long thought to be by Salvator
Rosa, it may indeed have been based on an idea of
his, as well as on a likeness made by a professional
portrait painter: the oil study for the head, recently
recovered for Kingston Lacy (No. 87B) would
support the latter part of this hypothesis, even
though the identity of its painter (who was not
Salvator Rosa) remains to be established.

72 After Sir GODFREY KNELLER Bt (1646/9–1723)
Mrs Voss (d. after 1716) with her daughter
Mrs Voss was Kneller's model and mistress, by
whom he had a daughter, Catherine (*c*.1690–1714),
who married James Huckle, a gentleman of Upper
(now West) Molesey, Surrey. The identification
rests on the tradition attached to John Smith's
mezzotint after the original of this painting of 1692
(shown in the South-East Dressing Room). Only
recorded here since the early nineteenth century.

73 Studio of Sir PETER LELY (1618–80)
Jane Needham, Mrs Myddelton (1645–92)
'That famous, & indeede incomparable beautifull
Lady' (Evelyn, *Diary*), and mistress of a succession
of lovers, from Charles II and his brother down-
wards. The comte de Grammont, however, claimed

the affectations and boredom of her conversation sent her lovers to sleep. The prime original is one of Lely's 'Windsor Beauties', in the Royal Collection.

74 After Sir ANTHONY VAN DYCK (1599–1641)
Prince Charles Louis (1617–80) and Prince Rupert of the Palatinate (1619–82)
The eldest surviving sons of the former King of Bohemia and Elizabeth, 'the Winter Queen', the eldest daughter of James I, visited London in 1635–7. Prince Rupert returned to command dashingly in the Civil War, and became a leading and civilising figure at Court after the Restoration. The original, once at Whitehall, is now in the Louvre.

75 Manner of TITIAN (*c.*1487/90–1576)
Omnia vanitas
Bought by William Bankes from the Marescalchi collection in Bologna in 1820, but previously in the Widmann collection in Venice. It seems to be the best of a number of versions of this composition, whose original author remains unknown, but who was clearly inspired by Titian's nudes. Its message appears to be that wealth, beauty, power – all is vanity.

76 After Sir ANTHONY VAN DYCK (1599–1641)
The three eldest children of Charles I
Prince Charles, later Charles II (b.1630); James, Duke of York, later James II (b.1633); Princess Mary, later Princess of Orange (b.1631). The original, of 1635, is at Windsor Castle.

77 JACOB HUYSMANS (*c.*1633–?96) after Sir ANTHONY VAN DYCK (1599–1641)
Cupid preparing his bow
Apparently based on Ovid's *Metamorphoses* (Book V, 355ff.), in which Cupid prepares to answer his mother Venus's summons to strike Pluto (here seen coasting around Sicily) with feelings of love through one of his arrows – which resulted in the Rape of Proserpine. This picture already belonged to Ralph Bankes in 1659. Van Dyck's original is in the Thyssen-Bentinck Collection.

78 After JOOS VAN CLEVE (active 1511–d.1540/1)
The Madonna and Child
Panel
Possibly the unattributed: 'A little Madonna wth A Saviour' in the collection of Ralph Bankes in 1659, as 'bought of Mr Henshaw'.

79 Imitator of PIETER HUYS (*c.*1519–81)
The Temptation of St Anthony
Panel
Ultimately derived from the various treatments of this demonic theme by Hieronymus Bosch (*c.*1450–1516), this is a later derivative of the less disturbing imitations of Bosch by Huys. St Anthony is shown twice: visited by disguised demons under a tree, and tormented by others in the air.

80 After PAOLO VERONESE (1528–88)
Two greyhounds
Copied from the dogs in Veronese's *Marriage at Cana* (Louvre), which was painted for the refectory of San Giorgio Maggiore in Venice. Given to William Bankes by the Prince of Anglona – as a Velázquez!

81 DUTCH, seventeenth-century
Head of Christ
Panel
This somewhat Rembrandtian or Carel Fabritius-like head appears to be the one simply listed amongst Ralph Bankes's pictures at Gray's Inn in 1659 as: 'Our Savior A small peice bought of mr Decreet [the painter-dealer Emanuel de Critz]'.

82 NETHERLANDISH, *c.*1600
A prophet with refugees fled from a village pillaged by soldiers
Panel
First recorded at Kingston Lacy, without attribution, in 1731.

83 ? VENETIAN, sixteenth-century
Head of a bearded man
Oil on paper laid down on panel
Just possibly 'A little head bought of N. Wray', valued at £5 in Ralph Bankes's 1659 Gray's Inn list.

84 SÉBASTIEN BOURDON (1616–71)
The Rape of Europa
An eclectic early work, apparently inspired by Domenichino or Gentileschi, and painted in Rome (1634–7), before Bourdon had forged the classicising Poussinesque manner of his maturity in Paris. Listed in Ralph Bankes's collection (along with No. 86, its pendant) in 1659.

85 ITALIAN, early seventeenth-century
Selene
The Greek goddess of the moon, identified as such by the crescent on her head, although the significance of the depiction is obscure. It seems to derive from a *Lucretia* attributed to Titian in the

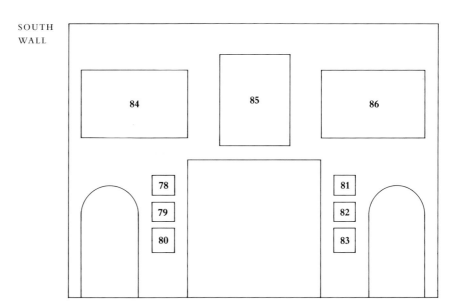

SOUTH WALL

Royal Collection, or from some common original. First recorded here in 1905.

86 SÉBASTIEN BOURDON (1616–71)
The Judgement of Midas
The pendant of No. 84, but more obviously in Bourdon's own manner.

129 N. WRAY (active *c*.1650–60) after Sir PETER LELY (1618–80)
*Anne Boteler, Countess of Newport, later Countess of Portland (*c*.1605/10–69)*
This portrait, the original of which is in the Clarendon Collection (on loan to Plymouth Art Gallery), has long been thought to show Lady Diana Russell, Viscountess Newport, and ultimately Countess of Bradford (1621/2–94); but the age of the sitter, and the prominent mole above her left lip, make it clear that it is of the Countess, formerly a prominent figure at the court of Charles I, and the wife of Mountjoy Blount, 1st Earl of Newport (*c*.1597–1665/6), like whom she had earlier been painted by Van Dyck (both at Petworth House, also NT). The copyist was himself painted by Lely (No. 61, Upper Landing). The picture was recorded in Ralph Bankes's collection at Gray's Inn before 1659.

155 FRANS SNYDERS (1579–1657) and Studio of Sir PETER PAUL RUBENS (1577–1640)
Cupid and Three Putti under a Garland of Fruit in a Landscape
Signed on the garland: *F. Snyders fecit*

Bought by William Bankes from the sale of the Altamira collection in London in 1827, and originally in that of the Marqués de Leganés (see p.73). The picture is one of a number of derivatives of one painted by Rubens and Snyders around 1615/20, of *The Infant Jesus with John the Baptist and two Child-Angels* now in the Kunsthistorisches Museum in Vienna (a good version of which is at Wilton House, Wiltshire, and a copy of that in pastels by Hoare of Bath at Stourhead, also NT). The essential theme, whether given a Christian or a pagan gloss, is a celebration of fertility.

156 GORTZIUS GELDORP (1553–1616/18)
Head of the Magdalen adoring the Cross
Geldorp (who was the father of the copyist of No. 62) made something of a speciality of lachrymose Magdalens, but, until this painting is cleaned, it is impossible to say whether it is an inferior but autograph replica, or a copy by another hand.

ON TABLES:

87 Sir GEORGE HAYTER, RA (1792–1871)
William John Bankes, MP (1786–1855)
Oil on millboard
Collector and traveller, rebuilt Kingston Lacy to Sir Charles Barry's designs 1835–40, and continued to orchestrate its decoration from exile abroad until his death. Study, 1836, for *Moving the Address to the Crown on the opening of the First Reform Parliament in*

the *Old House of Commons, 5 February 1833* (National Portrait Gallery). Hayter took ten years over the picture, making studies such as this of every MP bar one, which he offered to the subjects at ten guineas apiece afterwards. This is the only portrait in oils of William Bankes.

87A Sir WILLIAM CHARLES ROSS, RA (1794–1860)
Georgina Nugent, Mrs Bankes (1799–1875), and her three elder children, Georgina, Maria and Edmund
Miniature, watercolour on ivory. Signed on the reverse and dated 1830
Thought to be an illegitimate daughter of Ernest, Duke of Cumberland (later king of Hanover), she married George Bankes in 1822. Edmund succeeded to Kingston Lacy in 1856, but died only four years later at the age of 34. Ross was the last really successful British miniaturist, before photography destroyed the profession.

87B UNKNOWN ARTIST *c.*1680/90
Study for the head of Edward Altham (1622–94)
Oil on paper laid down on canvas
This picture was recorded (as by Salvator Rosa) at Kingston Lacy between 1731 and 1905, after which it unaccountably vanished. It reappeared at an auction at Christie's in 1968, with an 'antiqued' label purporting to identify it as a portrait of Alexander Pope by Richardson, only to disappear again and resurface in New York, whence it was bought back by the National Trust in 1995. Though a study for No. 70, this is clearly not a self-portrait, and is more sophisticated in execution than that is. The practice of making oil studies of heads on paper was both Flemish and Italian, but was not employed by Salvator Rosa, nor does the handling of this study seem Italian. Just possibly a study made by Michael Dahl (1656/9–1743) or Henry Tilson (*c.*1659–95), when they were in Rome in 1687/88.

FURNITURE

Most of the furniture dates from William Bankes's time.

The oak doors were made up from carving, some of which is, like the gilt dado rail, eighteenth-century French.

Anglo-Indian ebony settees, covered in floral cross-stitch embroidery generally known as Berlin work, but more correctly as overlaying work.

Pair of eighteenth-century Goanese ebony caskets on stands.

Composite Roman baroque giltwood console, on a bronzed base carved with crouching athletes, supporting a scalloped shell, dolphins and seated trumpeting tritons flanking a figure of Flora with a cornucopia. One of a pair intended for the Saloon.

Pair of Louis XIV Boulle pedestals or torchères, rebuilt in the nineteenth century. Part of a set now widely dispersed, others being at Stratfield Saye in Hampshire, Uppark in West Sussex, and in the Louvre.

Pair of nineteenth-century walnut marquetry centre-tables, made up with seventeenth-century cabinet doors for tops.

Charles II marquetry box on nineteenth-century stand, supplied in June 1838 by Nixon & Son of Great Portland Street for £12.

Four eighteenth-century Dutch or Portuguese colonial 'burgomaster' chairs, three of solid satinwood, one of ebony.

Nineteenth-century *contre-partie* Boulle *meuble d'entre deux*, with eighteenth-century ormolu plaques in the doors.

IN MARBLE NICHES:

Pair of eighteenth-century giltwood 'candelabra', a mermaid and a merman holding putti clasping cornucopia sprouting ormolu flowers for lights. William Bankes applied the tortoiseshell veneer to their triangular plinths, added the tortoises for feet and regilded them.

CARPET

Savonnerie carpet, decorated with a centre medallion and military trophies in the corners on an olive green ground. Said to have been made for St Cloud in 1814 and bought by Henry Bankes at the Fonthill Abbey sale in 1823. It is illustrated in Rutter's *Delineations of Fonthill and its Abbey* in the Grand Drawing Room.

CERAMICS

ON BOULLE PEDESTALS:

Pair of Paris porcelain flared stands with Egyptian caryatids and hieroglyphic decoration, *c.*1805.

IN WINDOWS:

Pair of large nineteenth-century Chinese blue-and-white jardinières on contemporary English stands.

ON CABINET:

Pair of nineteenth-century Chinese *famille rose* pheasants.

METALWORK

FLANKING FIREPLACE:

Pair of bronze firedogs supporting satyr- and sphinx-decorated candelabra, made in the Veneto in the sixteenth and nineteenth centuries. William

(Left) Egyptian Revival Paris porcelain flared stand with caryatid figures and hieroglyphs, c.1805 (Saloon)

Bankes put together late sixteenth-century Venetian bases with finer tops, perhaps by Severo da Ravenna (active in Padua, c.1500) and his workshop.

ON CHIMNEYPIECE:

Group of Venetian 16th-century bronze black-amoor heads which probably appealed to Bankes because the family crest is a moor's head with a cap of maintenance adorned with a crescent and a fleur-de-lis.

GLASS

George III chandelier, probably bought new by Henry Bankes in the 1780s. This is the 'noble lustre' mentioned by Frances Bankes in her account of the 1791 ball (see p.22).

The open doors allow another view of the Drawing Room, in which can be seen a small showcase containing Charles I's receipt for £525 for 25 horses from Sir John Bankes, and a miniature of William Bankes painted by George Sandars in 1812.

Continue round the Saloon via the chimneypiece wall to the Spanish Room on the left.

THE SPANISH ROOM

If William Bankes sought to leave his own monument for posterity, it is here in the 'Golden Room' or 'Spanish Picture Room' as he called it. He created it between 1838 and 1855 with consummate success as the rich and sombre, harmonious setting for the Spanish paintings acquired in his youth 40 years before.

This room was originally the Bedchamber to the Anteroom or Great Hall on Pratt's plan, with adjoining closets, as on the other corners of the house. In the 1780s it became the Eating Room, when Brettingham brought the great Dining Room, or Great Chamber (above the present Drawing Room), downstairs for Henry Bankes. This proved too small, but schemes to enlarge the room by Thomas Cundy (1820), Jeffry Wyatt (1821) and others were rejected on grounds of cost. In 1833 a block-like single bay was extended to the west, only to be demolished promptly after Henry's death the following year, when William adopted Barry's solution in the present Dining Room.

CEILING

The lavishly gilt and coffered ceiling reputedly came from a gallery in the Palazzo Contarini degli Scrigni, which the follower of Palladio, Vincenzo Scamozzi, added to the old Palazzo Contarini Corfu on the Grand Canal in Venice in 1609, but the paintings are actually copies of those from a ceiling in the Ca' Pisani that were sold in 1842 to the Kaiser-Friedrich Museum in Berlin (destroyed in 1945). William Bankes bought the ceiling and replica paintings (as originals, and from the Palazzo Contarini) from Town & Emanuel of 103 New Bond Street for £100, and adapted them to fit the Spanish Room in 1838–9.

The oval cartouches in the frieze, not from the same room, Bankes inscribed as labels for his paintings below. In 1854 he added the metal ropework, which was originally intended to frame tapestries in the Saloon.

LEATHER

Most of the tooled and painted leather that covers the walls came, in 1849, from another Palazzo Contarini near SS. Apostoli. A number of palazzi on the Grand Canal were once decorated in the same way, tapestries being less suitable for the humid climate. There was, however, not enough to cover the walls, and so Antonio Caldero was contracted to provide additional skins in 1852, having restored the old ones the year before. They were shipped to Britain in the brig *Marcolo Polo* in January 1853.

By the 1980s most of the leather had been reduced to a sorry state by light damage and discoloured varnish. Fortunately, the skins behind the paintings were in much better condition, and by conserving and rearranging these it has been possible to restore the original glowing beauty of the room.

DOORS

The three pairs of doors contain twelve pear wood panels painted between 1848 and 1851 with representations of the months by a Venetian artist, assisted by William Bankes himself and to his designs: 'They constitute, I believe, my best and certainly my largest work in drawing'. Bankes also gave detailed instructions for decorating the carved shutter panels, whose beading was to be gilded and burnished, 'always harmonising the gold with the ceiling'. The garlands of pendant fruit with flower swags were to receive 'a slight sprinkling of gold'.

SCULPTURE

The two panels of polychrome pendant garlands on either side of the chimneypiece were carved from marble probably taken from the Fabricotti quarries outside Florence. They were set against black marble from Belgium in 1855, supplied by Louis Roget.

AT FAR END OF ROOM:

Cabinet, faced with Florentine *pietra dura* panels, commissioned from the Buoninsegni brothers in 1850 to William Bankes's designs.

PICTURES

FROM CHIMNEYPIECE WALL, CLOCKWISE:

88 FRANCISCO RIBALTA (1565–1628)
Madonna and child with music-making angels
Bought by William Bankes in 1814 in Valencia, where it had been one of a number of paintings by Ribalta adorning the Goldsmith's Chapel of St Eligius in the parish church of St Catherine the Martyr.

89 Studio of FRANCISCO DE ZURBARAN (1598–1664)
St Justa
Typical of the female saints produced in series by Zurbaran and his studio in Seville, St Justa was usually paired with St Rufina. Patron saints of the city, they were daughters of a potter there, martyred for refusing to allow their father's vessels to be used in the worship of Venus. Bought by William Bankes in Spain in 1814.

90 ? SPANISH, early seventeenth-century
St Augustine of Hippo (354–430)
For the subject, see No. 17. Bought by William Bankes in Spain, with a provenance from 'Philibert, Duke of Savoy' (actually Emanuele Philiberto, 1588–1624, son of the duke, and ultimately Spanish Viceroy of Sicily), and then from the Cathedral at Placencia, as by 'Spagnolet' (Ribera). If, as is implied, Philibert gave the picture to the Cathedral of Placencia (there is no cathedral in Placencia), and since his career was spent in Italy rather than Spain, it is perhaps more likely that it is, if not by an Italian artist, by a Spanish painter working in Italy. Jusepe de Ribera (1588–1652) went to Italy when young, but at first worked largely on pictures for Spain. He dedicated an etching to Philibert in 1624.

The Spanish Room

91 JERÓNIMO JACINTO DE ESPINOSA (1600–67)
Don Francisco Vives de Cañamas, Conde de Faura
Bought by William Bankes in Spain in 1814. Espinosa evidently painted more than one whole-length portrait of the Vives family. They appear to have been disposed of by a 'widowed, half-mad Countess' who sold up the family house lock, stock and barrel, in order to move to Saragossa. The inspiration from Titian's portrait of *Charles V with his dog* now in the Prado seems evident.

92 Attributed to ALONSO CANO (1601–67)
The sleeping Christ Child
Bought by William Bankes in Spain, and regarded by him as 'a most delightful picture, it is in the very best manner of Alonso Cano, the next best of all the Spanish School to Velàsquez & Murillo; he was superior to either of them in drawing, particularly

of hands and feet.' But it is actually one of at least four known versions of this composition, all probably painted after Cano's return from Madrid to Granada in 1652.

93 After BARTOLOMÉ ESTEBAN MURILLO (1617–82)
Two peasant boys eating fruit
In Ralph Bankes's collection at Gray's Inn by 1659, as a copy, but still amongst the first examples of Spanish seventeenth-century painting to have been collected in England. The original is in the Alte Pinakothek, Munich.

94 Studio of FRANCISCO DE ZURBARAN (1598–1664)
St Elizabeth of Portugal (1271–1336)
Bought to replace the Velázquez portrait of *Philip IV* sold to Isabella Stewart Gardner in 1896. From a different series of female saints from No. 89 and arguably superior to that. St Elizabeth (or Isabella)

Don Francisco Vives de Cañamas, Conde de Faura; by Jerónimo Jacinto de Espinosa (No. 91; Spanish Room)

daughter took her vows, as the Dominican Sister Francesca Maria de Santa Rosa, the same year. St Rose was the first person from the Americas to be declared a saint. The miraculous vision is that, as shown here, when she was living in her parents' garden and doing needlework to help support them, the Christ Child appeared to her, seated on her work-basket, and invited her to be his bride. Bought, according to William Bankes, from the Marqués de Diezma (perhaps Ledesma).

96 PEDRO ORRENTE (1580–1645)
Moses and the burning bush
Bought by William Bankes in Granada, with its pendant, in order to have examples of this significant painter, whose works scarcely exist outside Spain. Moses's vision of God, in a 'bush that burned with fire and was not consumed' (*Exodus* iii, 2), was regarded as a prefiguration of the Virgin Birth.

97 PEDRO ORRENTE (1580–1645)
The Boy David and the lion
Pendant to No. 96, but acquired as 'Samson and the lion'. David was still a boy, and keeping his father's sheep, when he 'caught a lion by his beard, and smote him, and slew him' (I *Samuel* xvii, 34–5).

98 LUIS DE MORALES (*c.*1515/20–86)
Christ at the Column
From the convent of Atocha, Madrid. The Spanishness of Spanish painting really begins with Morales, and that is evidently why William Bankes wanted a work by him in his would-be representative collection of Spanish pictures. Known as 'the Divine' Morales for his copious production of religious images combining exquisite technique with insistent spirituality, the artist made a speciality of images of the suffering Christ.

99 Attributed to JUAN BAUTISTA MARTINEZ DEL MAZO (*c.*1612/15–67) after DIEGO VELÁZQUEZ (1599–1660)
'Las Meninas'
One of the most celebrated images in the history of Western art, this composition takes its name from the handmaidens of the Infanta Margarita (1651–73), daughter of Philip IV of Spain and Mariana of Austria, whom Velázquez depicts himself with, accompanied by two dwarves in the foreground, one of whom kicks the dog (reputedly a descendant of the Lyme mastiff given to Philip III) out of the way of the entering royal couple. Differences from the much larger original of 1656 now in the Prado (the omission of the reflections of the king and queen

of Portugal was canonised in 1626, shortly before this picture will have been painted. A great-niece of Elizabeth of Hungary/Thuringia, her *Vita* took on many of the elements of the latter's. These included the story, shown here, that when challenged by her brutal husband with wasting her substance on the poor, a miracle changed the scraps of food gathered in her dress into roses.

95 Studio of BARTOLOMÉ ESTEBAN MURILLO (1617–82)
St Rose of Lima (1586–1618)
Bears Murillo signature
The original is in the Museo Lázaro Galdiano in Madrid, and was painted around 1671, the year of Rose's canonisation, and possibly because Murillo's

in the mirror, and the reduction of the colours on the painter's palette) will have helped to convince Bankes, wrongly, that this was Velázquez's original sketch. It was in fact something almost equally rare: the then only copy of a masterpiece that was hidden from public view in the private apartments of the Royal Palace in Madrid. It was probably painted by Velázquez's son-in-law and successor as Painter to the Crown, and originally belonged to the supreme Spanish collector, Don Gaspar de Haro, Marquès del Carpio (cf. No. 101).

100 Formerly attributed to BARTOLOMÉ ESTEBAN MURILLO (1617–82)
A putto-angel holding something red: a fragment
According to William Bankes's own account to his father in 1815: 'The little Angel by Murillo was cut out by the French of one of his most famous pictures, the *Jubileo della Porciuncula* in the Capuchin convent at Seville.' The inscription on the cartouche that he had placed over the picture says, more picturesquely: 'cut out by the French soldiers & applied to the covering of a knapsack'. However, the little angel is not generally accepted as by Murillo, whose altarpiece of *St Francis's miraculous vision of the Jubilee conferred on the Chapel of the Portiuncula* is now in the Wallraf-Richartz-Museum in Cologne, lacking no such portion.

101 DIEGO VELÁZQUEZ (1599–1660)
Cardinal Camillo Massimi (1620–77)
The great patron, collector and friend of Poussin. Painted in his habit as a *cameriere segreto* (private chamberlain) of Pope Innocent X (who had appointed him this in 1646) during Velázquez's second visit to Italy (1649–50). Not only is such dress unusual in a portrait, but Velázquez has used ultramarine (ground lapis lazuli), something that was virtually never done in Spain. Sold by the Cardinal's heirs, and then in the collection of Don Gaspar de Haro, Marquès del Carpio (cf. No. 99), whilst he was in Italy (1682–7). Bought by William Bankes in 1820 from the Marescalchi collection in Bologna, and the finest of his Spanish pictures.

102 After DIEGO VELÁZQUEZ (1599–1660)
Cardinal Gaspar de Borja y Velasco (1582–1645)
A member of the family whose heads were Dukes of Gandia, but who are better known in their Italian manifestations as the Borgias. He was Cardinal-Protector of the Spanish Crown in Rome from 1611 to 1632, when forced to withdraw because of his opposition to Pope Urban VIII. Thereafter Arch-

bishop successively of Milan, Seville and finally Toledo (1643–5), when he was painted by Velázquez *gratis*, as the painter's application for nobility mentioned. No surviving version of Velázquez's portrait is generally accepted as the original, although this was reputedly given as such by a Borja, the Duchess of Gandia, to William Bankes in Spain.

CEILING PAINTINGS:

103a After PAOLO CALIARI, called IL VERONESE (1528–88)
The Creation of the Elements
Chronos (Time) in the centre, with his wife Cybele (Earth), and their children Zeus (Fire), Hera (Air) and Poseidon (Water).

103b, c *Putti with symbols*
For the complex history of the ceiling, see p.66. In Veronese's original these putti were arranged on all four sides of the centre, adjacent to the deity to whom their symbols related.

Christ before Pontius Pilate; miniature in the style of Simon Bening after Martin Schongauer, c.1525 (Spanish Room). It was in Ralph Bankes's collection by 1659

IN GILT CABINET:

The group of drawings and miniatures includes three which were in Ralph Bankes's possession in 1659: *Christ before Pontius Pilate*, in the style of Simon Bening (1483/4–1561) after Martin Schongauer (active 1469–d.1491), *c*.1525; *The Last Supper*, by a follower of Jean Bourdichon (?1457–?1521), *c*.1500; and *Mars and Venus*, the copy of a miniature by Peter Oliver (*c*.1594–1647) after a painting by Titian, then in the collection of the 10th Duke of Northumberland and now at Petworth in Sussex, which was damaged in the seventeenth century and converted to a *Nymph and Satyr*.

SCULPTURE

IN GILT CABINET:

After PAULUS VAN VIANEN (*c*.1570–1613)
Four gilt bronze plaquettes:

Apollo, Cupid and the dead Python

Jupiter sending Mercury to kill Argus

Mercury with the severed head of Argus and Juno inserting his eyes into the peacock's tail

Apollo pursuing Daphne transforming into a laurel

METALWORK

Pair of bronze firedogs topped by the figures of Mars, Venus and Cupid, from the workshop of Niccolò Roccatagliata (active 1593–after 1636).

FURNITURE

ON CABINET:

Eight-day striking mantel clock, signed by Francis Raynsford (*c*.1667–after 1704), 'a watch maker at Charing Cross', but actually made by Edward Appley (*c*.1656–88) about 1688. The clock was probably part of his stock passed on to Raynsford, who was in business after 1688.

AGAINST FIREPLACE WALL:

Four nineteenth-century chairs carved in the style of Daniel Marot (*c*.1660–1752).

BETWEEN WINDOWS:

Queen Anne pier-glasses, rebuilt for the room.

The George III-style dining-chairs and the gilt cabinet were added by Walter Ralph Bankes.

CERAMICS

Lambeth Delft blue-and-white punchbowl, painted with the Bankes coat of arms and the date 1707, one of the few objects at Kingston Lacy surviving from the elder John Bankes's time. It has a very early representation of a fox hunt.

CARPET

Axminster, purchased by Henry Bankes from Samuel Whitty around 1820. An Indian all-over design of flowers and foliage on a red ground.

Return to the Saloon, cross to the doors to the left of the marble niche, and turn left from the staircase landing into the State Bedroom.

THE STATE BEDROOM

In Pratt's layout of the 1660s this was the little parlour with a corner closet and small staircase to the basement, echoing the arrangements of at least one of the other three corner apartments on the principal floor. It must have been opened up by Brettingham in the 1780s to make the north parlour or Frances Bankes could not have sat so many people at supper for her ball in 1791. Barry subdivided it again in the 1830s, but the walnut cornice is eighteenth-century. The wallpaper is an Owen Jones design of the 1860s.

CEILING PICTURES

104a–d Studio of PAOLO CALIARI, called IL VERONESE (1528–88)
Allegory of Faith (central compartment) and three compartments with *Cupids, two carrying garlands, one carrying a spur and a clock*

104e Attributed to ALESSANDRO VAROTARI, called IL PADOVANINO (1588–1648)
Cupid with roses

104f–m FRANCESCO VASON
Eight Arabesque Panels
Certain of these arabesque panels were originally associated with the octagonal painting (No. 107, now over the Upper Marble Staircase) acquired by William Bankes from the Palazzo Grimani in Venice during its siege by the Austrians in 1849, but they were in a very bad state, and everything that one now sees seems to be the work of the Venetian painter William Bankes employed to restore and

complete them. The inset canvases must have come from at least two other different sources, since Bankes believed the *Allegory of Faith* and three of the *Cupids* to be by Paolo Veronese, but the other *Cupid* to be by Padovanino. The yoking is not inappropriate, however, since Padovanino was the first of many Venetian artists to revive the manner of Titian (as here) and Veronese.

OTHER PICTURES

ON CHIMNEYPIECE WALL:

MICHELANGELO MAESTRI (d.1812)
Mythological figures and cupids riding a variety of conveyances
Gouache over etched outlines
Other versions are inscribed by Maestri as having been done in Rome, after originals by Raphael's pupil and assistant, Giulio Romano (1499–1546). Maestri seems in fact to have been inspired by the similar vignettes which form part of the fresco decoration in the loggia of the Villa Madama on the outskirts of Rome. This was completed by Giulio

Romano after Raphael's death, although the actual fresco decoration was designed and executed by Baldassare Peruzzi and Giovanni da Udine (cf. ceiling over the Upper Marble Staircase, p.74).

On this and other walls there are also two watercolour *Scenes of Roman Piety* attributable to David Allan (1744–96), and watercolour copies of Veronese's *Alexander extending clemency to the family of Darius* (National Gallery); and of Bonifazio de' Pitati's (1487–1553) *Dives and Lazarus* in the Accademia in Venice; and of Titian and others' *Faith appearing to Doge Grimani* in the Doge's Palace.

BED

The 'state bedstead' was carved in walnut and holly, by Vincenzo Favenza in 1855, and was unfinished at William Bankes's death the same year. Some of the carved reliefs derive from antique or Baroque sources: for example, the central group of cupids is based on an engraving by Bartolozzi after G.B. Cipriani's drawing of an antique gem now in Boston; the Jupiter and Juno on a study by Annibale

The State Bedroom

Carracci for one of his frescoes in the Galleria Farnese, Rome, of about 1600. Among the other carved features are the Bankes coat of arms and bats along the headboard.

OTHER FURNITURE

Dutch seventeenth-century walnut seaweed marquetry cabinet-on-stand, made by Jan Roohals and I. Hoogeboom, who inscribed their names within.

PHOTOGRAPHS

Group photographs of the Kaiser's visit to Kingston Lacy in 1907, and that of the Princess of Wales in 1908; and of the late Ralph Bankes in naval uniform.

CERAMICS

ON CABINET:

Large garniture of three Delft blue-and-white late seventeenth-century octagonal baluster vases, painted with figures in the Chinese Transitional style. Possibly acquired by John Bankes the Elder.

TEXTILES

Nineteenth-century Windsor tapestry of *Europa and the Bull* purchased by W. R. Bankes.

THE STATE DRESSING ROOM (BATHROOM)

The ceiling is modelled on one at Inigo Jones's Queen's House, Greenwich. William Bankes wished the 'parquet floor for the Dressing Room to correspond in pattern with the compartments of the ceiling'.

CEILING PAINTING

VENETIAN, sixteenth-century and ENGLISH, late (?) nineteenth-century

105a–i *Venus in her chariot*
Fresco transferred to enlarged canvas, surrounded by eight ornamental panels
The ceiling was most probably made up after William Bankes's death, using elements that he had already sent back for the – abandoned – ceiling of the Library, together with the ruined survivor of a group of fresco fragments ascribed to Veronese

from the Palazzo Morosini in Venice that he had bought in London in 1838. It was awkwardly enlarged from a rectangle to a reduction of the octagon originally intended to take Tintoretto's painting of *Apollo and the Muses*. Curiously, whilst three of the corners contain ornamental versions of the Bankes fleur-de-lis, the fourth contains a monogram composed of the letters 'A' and 'B' – which were the maiden initials of William's sister, Lady Falmouth: Anne Bankes, who must have been dead by the time they were painted – or perhaps just repainted.

Return through the State Bedroom to the landing and climb the stairs.

THE UPPER MARBLE STAIRCASE

SCULPTURE

ON HALF-LANDING NEWEL:

Copy of a Roman marble candelabrum. The lizard on the plinth below was produced in 1848 by a carver named Moro who worked for Michelangelo Montresor in Verona.

OPPOSITE:

Baron CARLO MAROCHETTI (1805–67)
Pair of busts of Sir John Bankes (1589–1644)
Bronze
These may have been alternative ideas for an early form of William Bankes's Civil War pantheon in the Loggia. He originally intended the seventeenth-century Italian carved wood pedestals to support the serpent-handled bronze urns now on the terrace.

After JOSEPH NOLLEKENS (1737–1823)
William Pitt the Younger (1759–1806)
Plaster
Based on a death-mask. Pitt was a friend of Henry Bankes the Younger.

UNDER WINDOWS, BEHIND BALUSTRADE:

Copies of the sculpted frieze known as *The Borghese Dancers* in the Louvre, and of its pendant showing maidens adorning a candelabrum.

UNDER PAINTING:

Long relief of dancing putti, commissioned by William Bankes from one of his Italian craftsmen,

The Upper Marble Staircase

Pietro Lorandini, and compiled from works by Della Robbia and Donatello, executed in a special two-tone marble that is white on the surface and orange-red within.

The garlands of birds and fishes inset in the pilasters of the staircase are inscribed and dated 1846, and were carved by Salesio Angelo Pegrassi from William Bankes's own designs.

THE TOP LANDING

The top landing has three domes decorated with wreaths of bay and ribbons and the balustrade is of alabaster capped with Biancone.

SCULPTURE

ON BALUSTRADE:

Two candelabra in Biancone, carved after Bankes's sketch, *c.*1854.

The four bronze figures resting on green serpentine (*verde antico*) plinths are reduced, probably eigh-

teenth-century Florentine, versions of Michelangelo's monumental *Times of Day* in the Medici Chapel of S. Lorenzo in Florence.

PICTURES

106a, b FRANS SNYDERS (1579–1657) or PAUL DE VOS (*c.*1596–1678)

Hounds attacking a bull and Wolves attacking a horse

This pair of pictures was bought by William Bankes in 1827 from the sale of the Altamira Collection in London, as by the then more celebrated Frans Snyders. Count Altamira had inherited the vast collection of Diego Messia, Marqués de Leganés (?1580–1655),which included over fifty pictures by Snyders and others by Paul de Vos. Although they now appear almost square, they are actually upright compositions and were originally inset as such into the panelling of the Dining Room. The top 29 inches or so were folded over so as to fit them at the top of the stairs in the late nineteenth century. The plaster swags of produce around them must have been created at the same date.

107 Attributed to GIOVANNI DA UDINE
(1487–1561 or 1567)
Illusionistic trelliswork cupola with disporting putti
Bought by William Bankes from the Palazzo
Grimani by S. Maria Formosa in Venice in 1849. He
believed that it had been painted for Giovanni
Grimani, the Patriarch of Aquileia, in 1510, by
Giorgione, who would have done the putti, and by
Giovanni da Udine, his pupil, who did the birds and
foliage. Giovanni da Udine was indeed briefly
Giorgione's pupil, but he did not work in the
Palazzo Grimani for Patriarch Giovanni Grimani
until his return from Rome, in 1537–40. Giovanni
was famous for his ornament, but he also depicted
putti in a set of cartoons for tapestries woven for
Pope Leo X in Flanders, and was famous for the
illusionism of his depictions of natural history. Here
he combines these with daring perspectival effects in
the tradition of Mantegna.

FURNITURE

George III black and gold chinoiserie lacquer
cabinet on stand.

William and Mary marquetry longcase clock, by
Francis Raynsford.

Turn left into the South-East Bedroom.

THE SOUTH-EAST
BEDROOM

'Bedroom No. 1' has been redecorated by the Trust,
after the eradication of severe dry rot, with a
wallpaper design of about 1840–50.

PICTURES

108 RICHARD ROPER (active *c.*1735–*c.*1775)
Margaret Wynne, Mrs Bankes (1724–1822) *and
her daughter Anne* (b.1759)
Daughter of Dr John Wynne, Bishop of Bath and
Wells, who acquired Soughton in Flintshire.
Second wife of Henry Bankes the Elder, 1753. Anne
became an amateur copyist in pastel, doing the
Infant Samuel receiving the call in the Bedroom
Corridor.

132 JACOB DE WIT (1695–1754)
Putti enacting an Allegory of Summer
Signed: *J.d. Wit/1739*
A late acquisition. De Wit specialised in illusionistic
paintings such as this, simulating white plaster
reliefs, as overmantels and overdoors.

110 RICHARD ROPER (active *c.*1735–*c.*1775)
Henry Bankes the Elder, MP (1698–1776)
Signed and dated 1764 on the back
Younger brother of John Bankes (No. 10), whose
neglect of the family estates he repaired. Fellow of
King's College, Cambridge, 1723–9, and barrister.
Succeeded his brother as MP for the family seat,
Corfe Castle, 1741–62; but surrendered his seat for
a Commissionership of Customs.

128 ENGLISH, *c.*1730
Dr John Wynne, Bishop of Bath and Wells
(1667–1743)
Father of Margaret Wynne, the second wife of
Henry Bankes the Elder. Nominated to the see of St
Asaph in 1714/5, he was translated to the Bishopric
of Bath and Wells in 1727. In 1732 he purchased
Soughton in Flintshire; this and his wealth were
inherited in 1815 by his great-grandson, William
Bankes, who gave a three-quarter-length version of
this portrait to Jesus College, Oxford, of which the
sitter had been President.

112 JOHN JAMES BAKER (active *c.*1690–1710)
Sir Henry Parker of Honington, 2nd Bt, MP
(*c.*1640–1713)
Oval
Nephew and successor, by special remainder, of the
1st Bt, Sir Hugh, a London merchant, he married
Margaret Hyde (No. 116) in 1665. His daughter
Margaret married John Bankes the Elder in 1691,
the same year as her elder sister Frances (No. 117)
was married to Sir John Pakington, when these
portraits were possibly painted for John Bankes and
his wife. The Parkers of Honington were a junior
line of the Parkers of North Molton, Devon, whose
senior line rose to become the Earls of Morley, of
Saltram. From the Honington line, in turn, descend
the Hyde Parkers of Melford Hall, Suffolk, in
whose family the baronetcy continues to this day.

113 ENGLISH, *c.*1700
Miss Margaret Pakington (b.1691 or after)
Oval. Inscribed on the back: '*Miss Margaret
Pakington*'
Almost certainly a daughter of Sir John Pakington,
4th Bt, and Frances Parker (No. 117), who married

in 1691. Her mother's sister, Margaret Parker, Mrs John Bankes, would have been her godmother, after whom she would have been named, and to whom this portrait would have been given. Recorded with this identity, but no attribution, from the 1762 inventory onwards, in association with No. 115. Possibly by the same mysterious 'Thredder', but if so, painted separately.

114 THREDDER, 1702
John Bankes the Elder, MP (1665–1714)
Oval
Son of Sir Ralph Bankes, married Margaret Parker in 1691. Inscribed with his identity and dated 1702 on the reverse, and recorded in 1762 (and possibly in 1731) as by this otherwise unknown artist. Apparently spelled thus in the 1731 list, but if this was a misreading, then it is most likely to be by William Reader (fl.1672–after 1700), who is recorded by Vertue as having 'liv'd at a noblemans house in the West of England, sometime'.

115 THREDDER, 1702
John Bankes the Younger as a Boy (1692–1772)
Oval
Like No. 114, inscribed and dated 1702, and similarly attributed in the 1762 inventory and the 1731 list (where spelled 'Threader'). With No. 113, they were hung in John Bankes's Closet in 1762, along with most of the other small and precious pictures.

116 JOHN JAMES BAKER (fl.1690–1710)
Margaret Hyde, Lady Parker (d.1728/9)
Oval
Daughter of Dr Alexander Hyde, Bishop of Salisbury (1598–1667), a staunch Royalist, first cousin of Clarendon (No. 35, Dining Room), and father of Robert Hyde (No. 131, Upper Staircase). Married in 1665 to Sir Henry Parker of Honington, 2nd Bt (No. 112), and mother of John Bankes the Elder's wife, Margaret (?No. 119), and of Frances, Lady Pakington (No. 117).

117 JOHN JAMES BAKER (active c.1690–1710)
Frances Parker, Lady Pakington (1670/1–before 1700)
Oval
Daughter of Sir Henry Parker, 2nd Bt (No. 112) and Margaret Hyde (No. 116), and sister of Mrs John Bankes the Elder (No. 119). She was married in 1691 to Sir John Pakington, 4th Bt, MP (1671–1727) of Westwood, Worcestershire.

118 JOHAN ZOFFANY (1733–1810)
The Woodley Family
William Woodley, MP (1728–93) was twice Governor of the Leeward Islands (1766–71 and 1792–3) and Lt-Governor of Antigua (1768–88 and 1792–3). His elder daughter Frances (No. 29) married Henry Bankes the Younger in 1784. She is shown offering a rose to the newest-born child, John (1766–95), who died when his ship, HMS *Leda*, capsized in a squall off Madeira. The older boy is William (1762–1810), later President of St Kitts and Lt-Governor of Berbice. The seated child is Harriet, who married Thomas Pickard of Bloxworth in 1788, and became an amateur artist in pastels (see those in the Bedroom Corridor, p.78, and the White Dressing Room, pp.80–81).

119 ? HENRY MORLAND (active c.1675–c.1708)
? *Margaret Parker, later Mrs John Bankes* (after 1665–1730)
Previously inscribed on the reverse: *Miss Margaret Parker*
Daughter of Sir Henry Parker, 2nd Bt (No. 112), and Margaret Hyde, Lady Parker (No. 116), who married John Bankes the Elder (No. 114) in 1691. This could be the portrait of her by 'Moreland' listed in 1731 as *'Miss Parker'*, which suggests that it was a portrait of her as a young girl, as this is.

120 ENGLISH, c.1680–90
? *Frances Bankes* (1697–1709) *as a shepherdess*
Previously inscribed on the back: *Miss Frances Bankes*
Apparently a younger daughter of John Bankes the Elder (No. 114) and his wife Margaret Parker (?No. 119), but the style and costume seem too early for it to be of any of their children. It is possible that the inscription was put on later and was mistaken.

FURNITURE

Painted mahogany bed with painted cornice *en suite* with the curved window cornices of the 1790s. Rehung in 1991.

Suite of four eighteenth-century mahogany chests of drawers, perhaps from Ince & Mayhew. (Two are in the Dressing Room.)

Painted oval pier-glass, c.1770.

TEXTILES

Eighteenth-century Anglo-Indian embroidered silk bedspread.

Worsted Brussels fitted carpet, rewoven in 1991 from a fragment dating from before 1850, found in a neighbouring bedroom.

THE CABINET ROOM

Recently a bathroom, this has one of Barry's coved and decorated plaster ceilings.

PICTURES

OVER DOOR TO DRESSING ROOM:

124 ? JAN PORCELLIS, known as PORCELLIS THE ELDER (1587–1632)
Shipping off a coast in rough seas
Very possibly the picture listed as '*A Storme of Porcellis*' in Ralph Bankes's list of his pictures at Gray's Inn in 1659, but reframed in the nineteenth century. The taste for Porcellis's paintings in England seems to have been established by Charles I, who owned several, three of which survive at Hampton Court.

TO LEFT OF CABINET, FROM TOP:

D9 Attributed to JACQUES BLANCHARD (1600–38)
Recto: *The Drunkenness of Noah*
Brown wash over red chalk
Verso: *Sketch of a sculpted ornamental feature*
Red chalk
Although this and the following drawing are both inscribed in an apparently seventeenth-century hand '*Diseg: di Mons. Posin*' and '*di mano propria*' ('by his own hand'), they are not by Poussin, but by another French artist working in his orbit in Italy. The likeliest candidate is Blanchard, who went to Rome in 1624 (like Poussin), but spent from 1626 to 1628 in Venice, whence these and the small group of drawings to which they belong seem to have come.

D1 Attributed to JACQUES BLANCHARD (1600–38)
Recto: ? *Venus and Mars in a bedchamber with Cupid*
Brown wash and red chalk
Verso: *Selene and the sleeping Endymion*
Brown wash and red chalk

D2 Sir PETER LELY (1618–80)
? *Head of a Young Woman of the Packington family*
Coloured chalks on buff paper
The identity of the sitter is uncertain, and this is anyway very possibly a study of a 'Beauty' done for

Thomas Betterton the Actor as Solyman in Davenant's 'Siege of Rhodes'; chalk drawing by John Greenhill, 1663 (No. D3; Cabinet Room)

its own sake. First recorded as one of the precious pictures 'in my brother's Closet', in Henry Bankes's 1762 inventory of John Bankes's collection at Kingston Hall, as just 'a Lady', but when Sir William Musgrave visited Kingston Hall in 1797, he was told that she was 'Mrs Packington', and on a recently rediscovered picture list (but of *c*.1800) she is called 'Miss Packington'.

D3 JOHN GREENHILL (*c*.1644/5–76)
Thomas Betterton the Actor (?1635–1710) as Solyman in Davenant's 'Siege of Rhodes'
Black and red chalk, signed and dated 1663
Also first recorded 'in my brother's Closet' in 1762, but as 'Betterton the Player in the Character of Bejazet, in Crayons by Sir Peter Lilly'. Greenhill was Lely's most individual pupil; he mingled with actors, and was the first British artist to portray them in character.

121 GASPAR DE WITTE (1624–81)
A rocky wooded landscape with a figure on a path
Panel. Signed: G.D./WITTE F.
Ralph Bankes evidently had a fondness for landscape painting, but only this picture and the great Berghem (No. 69) survive at Kingston Lacy.

TO RIGHT OF CABINET, FROM TOP:

D5 NORTH ITALIAN, c.1600
The Magdalen annointing Christ's feet in the house of Simon
Pen, brown ink and wash
Inscribed on the former mount: *Desegno de Paolo a Veronese mani propria.*

TO LEFT OF SOUTH WINDOW, FROM TOP:

H. EGLETON after A. E. CHALON, RA (1780–1860)
Anne Frances Bankes, Countess of Falmouth (1789–1864)
William Bankes's much-loved sister, who intermittently occupied this apartment after the death of her husband in 1841.

ENGLISH, c.1820
View of Tregothnan from the sea
Watercolour
Tregothnan in Cornwall was rebuilt in Tudor style for Anne Frances's husband, the 4th Viscount (later 1st Earl) of Falmouth, after their marriage in 1810, by William Wilkins, 1816–18.

ENGLISH, c.1820
River scene, with a bridge and rocks
Watercolour

TO RIGHT OF SOUTH WINDOW:

WARNER GYSELMAN (Belgian, nineteenth-century)

122 *View of a path and meadows, with sheep*

123 *View of a path with a hut by a stream*

Panels, both signed
Not recorded at Kingston Lacy until this century, and scarcely worthy of it.

OVER DOOR TO SOUTH-EAST BEDROOM:

D4 LELIO ORSI (1511–87)
Recto: *Design for a frieze*
Verso: *Kneeling Saint holding a boy*
Pen, brown ink and wash, over black chalk
Inscribed in graphite in a later hand in the cartouche: *Lelio di Novellaria/F.1546*, and with the collector's mark of 1st Earl Spencer (1734–83).

Orsi was one of the most bizarre and imaginative draughtsmen of the sixteenth century, working for, and on terms of friendship with, a cadet branch of the Gonzaga family established in Novellara. The inscription is misleading, since the juxtaposition of the ornament of Roman Imperial architecture on the left-hand side, with that of the palace of Fontainebleau on the right, probably points to a date in the 1560s.

D6–8 GIACOMO FRANCO (1556–1620)
Three scenes during the Venetian Carnival
Pen, brown ink and wash
These three drawings were all engraved (anonymously) in reverse for Giacomo Franco's *Habiti d'Huomeni et Donne Venetiane* (1610) as the *Ordine . . . nel dare il bastone all' Ecc.ᵐᵒ General di Mare, Le feste del giovede Grasso,* and the *Battaglio dei pugni a San Barnaba.*

CERAMICS

FURNITURE

Eighteenth-century cabinet on stand, of padouk-wood inlaid with ivory, Vizagapatam, Anglo-Indian.

CERAMICS

Large Ming Kraak porcelain charger, c.1610.

THE SOUTH-EAST DRESSING ROOM

PICTURES

The pictures in this room are a *mélange* of old oil paintings (reflecting its past use as a picture store); drawings; watercolours, including three views and a reconstruction of Corfe Castle; and engravings, particularly of pictures in the collection. The more interesting include:

LEFT OF DOOR FROM CABINET ROOM:

111 ENGLISH, mid-eighteenth-century
Unknown Young Man in bottle-green
Painted oval
The unknown sitter may be dressed for hunting. The artist is close to Thomas Hudson, who gave his opinion on the four *Evangelists* now attributed to Seghers (Nos 6, 8, 15, 17).

REGINALD EVES (1876–1941)
Ralph Bankes (1902–81)
Black chalk. Signed and dated 1924
The donor to the National Trust on his death of the estates of Corfe Castle and Kingston Lacy. Drawn by a society artist who painted another Dorset man, Thomas Hardy.

GOTTFRIED SAITER after VALENTIN LEFEBVRE (*c*.1642–*c*.1680)
Omnia vanitas
Engraving after Lefebvre's drawing of the painting then ascribed to Titian now in the Saloon (No.75). From a set of engravings after Lefebvre published in 1682.

JOHN SMITH after Sir GODFREY KNELLER (1646/9–1723)
Mrs Voss and her daughter
Mezzotint of 1692 after the original of the painting now in the Saloon (No. 72). Although the print is not inscribed with the names of the sitters, the tradition that it shows Kneller's mistress and their child is of long standing.

ABOVE OVERMANTEL MIRROR:

127 The Hon. HENRY GRAVES (1818–82)
Florence Mary Anne Fane, Mrs Albert Bankes
Signed and dated 1877
Painted four years after her marriage in 1873 to Wynne Albert Bankes (1840–1913) of Wolfeton, Dorset, the fourth son of the Rt Hon. George Bankes, MP, and Georgina Charlotte Nugent. Lent by the Countess Zamoyska.

125 FLEMISH, *c*.1600
Christ rebuking St Peter
In *Matthew* xvi, 23 Christ rebukes Peter with the words 'Get thee behind me, Satan', for attempting to deny that he would be crucified.

126 LAURA HOPE, née TROUBRIDGE (1858–1929)
Walter Ralph Bankes (1853–1904)
Pastel
The father of the donor of Kingston Lacy, which he inherited at the age of sixteen.

Laura Hope was a daughter of Sir Thomas Troubridge, Bt, ADC to Queen Victoria, and the wife of Adrian Hope, a descendant of the Earls of Linlithgow, and joint guardian of Oscar Wilde's children. A command to paint twenty-two of Queen Victoria's grandchildren made her artistic reputation at a stroke, while her 'beauty and poise made her the doyenne of Hyde Park's society cyclists'. Her sister-in-law was none other than Una, Lady Troubridge, the lifelong companion of the lesbian novelist Radclyffe Hall.

THE BEDROOM CORRIDOR AND ATTIC STAIRCASE

The barrel vault and coffered ceiling belong to Brettingham's alterations for Henry Bankes in the 1780s. At the end of the Corridor is Barry's ingenious apse leading to bathrooms and bedrooms and lit by carefully contrived natural light from the alabaster shells and fanlights. At the top is Barry's six-sided cupola with its frieze of baroque swags of fruit suspended from lion masks. On either side of the lantern are two plaster wreaths of fruit and ribbons.

PICTURES

ON LEFT- AND RIGHT-HAND WALLS:

Similarly framed pastels after paintings by Sir Joshua Reynolds (1723–92): a *Self-portrait* of the artist; a *Girl resting on a ledge*, by Mrs Pickard; and an *Infant Samuel receiving the call*, recorded after 1772 as by 'Miss Bankes' presumably Anne (b.1759; see No. 108), the daughter of Henry Bankes the Elder, who had come into the Kingston Lacy estate that year.

ON RIGHT-HAND WALL:

133 ? FRANCIS CLEYN THE ELDER (?1582–1657/8)
John Bankes (1626-56) *and Sir Maurice Williams, his tutor*
First recorded *c*.1656, and described in the note of Ralph Bankes's pictures in Gray's Inn of *c*.1658 as: 'My Brothers Picture & Sr M. Williams. A long Cloth by Decline.' Cleyn is best known as chief designer to the Mortlake tapestry works, but both he and his son are also recorded as painting portraits, though none has hitherto been definitively identified.

131 ENGLISH, *c*.1690
Robert Hyde of West Hatch
First mentioned in 1731, and listed in 1762 as a portrait of 'Robert Hyde of West Hatch in Wiltshire Esq.', this must be a portrait of the brother of Margaret Hyde, Lady Parker (cf. No. 116, South-East Bedroom), head of the senior lines of the Hydes. 'West Hatch' would seem to be the now

much altered Hatch House, Newtown, near Tisbury.

109 RICHARD ROPER (active *c.*1735–*c.*1775)
John Bankes the Younger, MP (1692–1772)
Signed and dated: *R^d Roper Pinx^t 1764*
This three-quarter-length portrait was evidently done from the same sitting as No. 10, although the pose is reversed.

THE UPPER LANDING

PICTURES

TO LEFT:

61 Sir PETER LELY (1618–80)
N. Wray (active *c.*1650–60)
Painter, copyist and dealer employed by Ralph Bankes, who owned this portrait of him by 1659.

134 FLEMISH, early seventeenth-century
The Tribute Money
From its early frame, most probably one of the pictures acquired by Ralph Bankes, even though not recorded in 1659. It was rediscovered around 1854, tucked behind another painting. Certain details – notably the old Levite in spectacles craning forward at the left – seem to have been inspired by Rubens's three-quarter-length version of this subject, now in the Fine Arts Museum, San Francisco, but first recorded in the collection of William of Orange. Possibly by the same artist as the *Christ rebuking St Peter* (No. 126, South-East Dressing Room).

STRAIGHT AHEAD:

135 After HENDRIK GOLTZIUS (1558–1617)
The Circumcision
Copied from an engraving done in imitation of Dürer, but with Goltzius's signature suppressed, and the date changed from 1594 to 1607. Apparently, as its eighteenth-century frame would support, acquired by Henry Bankes the Elder, who ascribed it to 'Old Franks'.

ON RIGHT-HAND SIDE:

71 Follower of FRANS FLORIS I (1516–70)
Faith, Hope and Charity
One of a pair of panels in the manner of this artist at Kingston Lacy; the other awaits restoration. First recorded here in 1731, but it is in a mid-seventeenth-century frame characteristic of the collection.

THE TENT ROOMS

On the south and east sides, the tented attic rooms were bachelor bedrooms, whereas the servants' bedrooms (now a flat and storerooms) were on the north side. Two of the three Tent Rooms (beyond the research library) have been restored. They date from 1835–41 and continue the fashion of Empress Josephine's Malmaison near Paris, and the Charlottenhof at Potsdam. In 1841 they contained furniture from the main rooms, which were still in the hands of the builders. In 1856 they were modestly furnished with painted washstands and dressing-tables. The carved ebonised bedstead, like the others, was dressed in 'striped merino bed furniture'.

PICTURES

For over a century, the upper parts of Kingston Lacy have been used to store pictures that were either no longer thought worthy of, or not in a suitable condition to be hung in, the main rooms of the house. The National Trust is still grappling with this legacy, and so these areas will continue to be used for pictures awaiting restoration, or for those recently restored, but awaiting proper study and possible allocation elsewhere in the house. Room stewards will have up-to-date lists of what is on view.

Return and descend to the second floor, turning left into

THE WHITE BEDROOM, BATHROOM AND DRESSING ROOM

These were furnished for or after the marriage of Henrietta Fraser to W. R. Bankes in 1897, but bills have not been found for the white painted furniture. On the walls are French and English engravings, and photographs of Mrs Bankes and her children.

CERAMICS

ON MANTELPIECE:

Two Daoguang (1825–50) yellow-ground bowls, typical of the porcelain looted from the Summer Palace in Peking by French and British troops in 1860.

The White Bedroom

CARPET

Probably Indian, with bands of ribbons within a border. The technique is Persian knot, with cotton warp and jute weft.

PICTURES

The pictures here are primarily prints. In the White Bedroom there is one watercolour of an as yet unidentified young woman, by Mary Gow (1851–1929)

All the pictures in the White Dressing Room are in pastel, with the exception of a small portrait in oils of *Daphne Bankes* (b.1898) by a painter apparently signing himself 'Annigani', and another watercolour by Mary Gow, of *Henrietta Fraser, Mrs Walter Bankes* (d.1953). Three of them are – like those in the Corridor – by Henry Bankes the Elder's daughter, Anne (b.1759), and by Frances Woodley's sister, Harriet Pickard, who seems, from the

similarity of their productions, to have been her teacher, after oil paintings by, or prints after, other artists.

ON BEDROOM WALL:

FRANCIS COTES (1726–70)
Portrait of a young girl
Painted oval
Signed *FCotes 175[9?]*

ON BATHROOM WALL:

? ANNE BANKES after ? Sir JOSHUA REYNOLDS, PRA (1723–92)
Head of an infant
Oval

HARRIET WOODLEY, Mrs PICKARD after JEAN-BAPTISTE GREUZE (1725–1805)
La fille en extase
After a picture successively in the collections of Louis XIV's extravagant finance minister Calonne

(1734-1802), and of Robert Smith, 1st Baron Carrington (1752–1838).

Mrs PICKARD after WILLIAM HOARE of
BATH (1707–92)
Summer
Known also as *Lady out of the Bath.*

Descend to the bottom of the staircase for the Audit Room on the right and turn left before the great fireplace in the Hall to leave the house by the Back Hall, the Egyptian Collection in the Billiards Room, and the Servants' Hall.

THE BACK HALL

It contains the well-stocked butler's silver cupboard and some fine eighteenth-century dress swords by the best London and Paris sword-makers. Nearby was the Muniment Room which housed the Bankes family archives, now on deposit in the County Record Office in Dorchester.

BANKES LEAF

The dramatic discovery of the Bankes, or Coelfrith, Leaf came from papers found in a damp box in the boot room. Written in Northumbria in the early eighth century, it is part of a Bible made at Wearmouth/Jarrow in Abbot Coelfrith's time and described by the Venerable Bede. The Bible was probably destroyed at the Reformation, but a number of fragments survived which are now in the British Library and have been joined by the Bankes Leaf on loan. A facsimile is shown here.

THE EGYPTIAN COLLECTION

The adjacent room, formerly the housekeeper's room and since 1930 the Billiards Room, is arranged to display William Bankes's Egyptian collection (see Chapter Four) and to disprove Johann Burckhardt's warning to him 'not to bury your treasures at your country house where they can never generally be admired'.

The small antiquities are of great beauty and interest, but few have any provenance. They include a schist cosmetic palette in the form of a fish (earlier than 3000BC), small bronze cats, cockerels and figures of the leonine dwarf god Bes, faience

Egyptian stela, or tomb inscription, from Deir el-Medina. Huy offering to Amen-re, Mut and a lion-headed goddess, with a family procession below

scarabs (sacred beetles) and *amulets* (protective charms), together with a good collection of *shabtis* (mummy figures), who were deputies assigned to carry out tasks for the dead in the after-life, such as restoring the land after the annual floods.

The collection of 25 *stelae* (tomb inscriptions) comes from the workmen's village at Deir el-Medina, situated within the great necropolis west of the Nile which served the important cult and administrative centre of Thebes in Upper Egypt. These were the craftsmen who made the royal tombs in the Valley of the Kings, among others, and worshipped not only the great Theban gods, but also others from further afield, suggesting some were of distant origin. One *stela* depicts two chisel-bearers.

The four fragments of tomb paintings come from an unidentified tomb of the period 1425–1375BC in the Theban necropolis. The ritual scenes depicted, typical of an XVIIIth Dynasty tomb, are of banquets with eating, drinking, music and dancing, in which the tomb-owner would hope to take part in his after-life. These include harpists, a lute player and a lively group of girl musicians, accompanied by the presentation of offerings to the deceased and a man offering braziers with cooking ducks.

The fine free-standing greywacke figure of a striding male god with the features of Rameses II of the XIXth Dynasty was found face-down in the fernery. He is incised on the back column with an invocation and may be dated about 1235BC, but is of unknown provenance.

THE SERVANTS' HALL

PICTURES

On the outer face of the partition between the Back Hall and the Servants' Hall is a number of oil sketches on board by Alec Cobbe, showing pictures being rehung at Kingston Lacy in 1985.

138–40 THOMAS G. TARGETT (active 1869–81)
Dead duck and hare; Dead trout; Dead pike
Signed and dated 1881

127 ? SPANISH, seventeenth-century
A royal child seated by a vase of flowers and a monkey with a garden beyond

141–2 NETHERLANDISH, seventeenth-century
Wooded landscapes with ruins
These, and probably all the other large landscapes in this room, were first recorded in 1731, and again in 1762 relegated to the Great Staircase.

? ITALIAN, early seventeenth-century
Four architectural capricci of Ancient Rome, with figures
Survivors of a set of six such pictures first recorded in 1731, and in 1762 as hung in two groups of three on the Great Staircase, with these titles:

143 *The Middle Part of the Circus Maximus* [?]

144 *Two Temples, one of Honour, the other of Virtue*

145 *Vespasian's Amphitheatre with the Columna Rostrata*

146 *The Tomb of Augustus Caesar* [actually *The Appian Way*]

147 NETHERLANDISH, seventeenth-century
A wooded landscape with a milkmaid milking a cow and labourers outside a farm building

148–9 ENGLISH, first half of the seventeenth century
A pair of views of the Thames, with the old palaces of Greenwich and Whitehall
These – apparently unique – early views of the two royal palaces are first recorded at Kingston Lacy in 1731, but were probably collected by Ralph Bankes. They may be copies of lost paintings by Cornelis Bol (active 1607–66), a topographical painter who was recorded in London 1635/6. The view of Greenwich contains the earliest known and most complete depiction of Henry VIII's palace, Placentia.

150 FLEMISH or FRENCH, early seventeenth-century
A Cook with a still-life of vegetables and game
First recorded in 1731, evidently – as in 1762 – in an honourable position in the Great Hall, before it was relegated to the Servants' Hall. There was a vogue for such depictions at the beginning of the seventeenth century, and the earliest and most capable English amateur artist, Sir Nathaniel Bacon (?1583–1627), is thought to have produced some.

151 NETHERLANDISH, mid-seventeenth-century
A wooded landscape with gravediggers

152 NETHERLANDISH, early seventeenth-century
A wooded landscape with herdsman, cattle and goats, watched over by a dog

153 ENGLISH, early nineteenth-century
A mountainous wooded river landscape with an angler

THE KITCHEN COURTYARD

The eighteenth-century Kitchen Courtyard was designed by William Rice (c.1734–89), Surveyor of Buildings to HM Customs, for Henry Bankes the Elder in 1775-6, with the laundry and drying room on the south (left-hand) side. The north range was enlarged in the 1780s by Brettingham for Henry Bankes the Younger's kitchen, which now contains the shop. The sculleries and storerooms have been thrown together to make an education room. Beyond lies the stable range of 1882 where the tea-room has been installed.

CHAPTER NINE
THE GARDEN AND PARK

No plan or illustration of Sir Ralph Bankes's garden in the 1660s has yet come to light. But its character can have changed little during the next 100 years, for his son, John the Elder, had no spare money until near the end of his life, and his long-lived grandson, bachelor John, was as conservative in his gardening taste as in everything else. So William Woodward's plan of 1774-5, drawn a couple of years after John's death, provides invaluable evidence of the early formal garden, and by taking away later additions it is possible to reconstruct Sir Ralph's original layout.

Immediately south of the house he placed the walled Parterre Garden, a rectangular area divided by gravel paths and low hedges into four lawns or parterrres (flower-beds), with a statue in each. This was flanked to the east and west by two smaller compartments of nearly equal size, for evergreens, fruit trees and flowers; and at the southern end of the layout, beyond a terraced cross-walk, the sym-metrical design was completed by a walled *exedra*, in which ten statues or urns were set in a semicircle to terminate the vista from the house. Somewhere on the edge of this garden Sir Ralph built a raised pavilion or belvedere with a view out over the park; though always referred to as the 'banqueting house', it was really a comfortable room away from the noise and bustle of the mansion, where family and friends could withdraw on a summer evening. It was finally pulled down in 1721.

On the north side he had to be content with a modest entrance court looking out into Court Close, an area of ancient unimproved parkland. But on the south, in Upper Park, he must have planted the walks radiating from the *exedra*, because after the Great Storm of November 1703 – a storm as

devastating over southern England as those of 1987 and 1990 – one of the clearance gangs spent six weeks 'raising of trees in the walks blown down with the violent wind'. Other more functional features, such as stables, kitchen garden and orchard, were placed on convenient sites away from obvious view.

In 1713, when money at last became available, improvements were undertaken in the garden. Decayed stonework was replaced and ornamental features added, such as new tubs for exotics and 'lead flower pots' (urns or planters), some of which

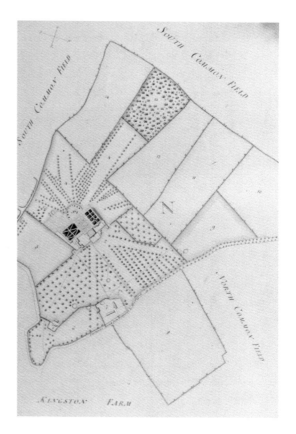

(Right) Woodward's 1774–5 plan provides evidence of the early formal layout around Sir Ralph Bankes's house. It is one of 50 he made of the Bankes estates

The south lawn as laid out by William Bankes with
Italian well-heads and other garden sculpture; engraving
by Philip Brannon from Hutchins's 'Dorset' (1868)

remarkably were gilded. A bowling green was
made on the east side, though it seems soon to have
been absorbed into the enlarged East Wilderness,
whose criss-cross, diagonal paths can be clearly seen
on Woodward's plan. The north side was taken in
hand in 1716-17, when 146 elms were planted in
Court Close.

Further improvements took place on the north
side in 1733–4. 'William Oliver and his men' rebuilt
the walls of the entrance court, for which Mr
Greenway of Bath supplied a pair of Bath stone
vases for £2 12s 6d, and this remodelled entrance
front was illustrated in Hutchins's *Dorset* (1774).
Gangs of labourers spent several weeks over the
winter of 1733–4 'Rooting up the two inner Rows
of Elms' to make a central vista across Court Close,
where a statue was set up on the main axis, and in
1734–5 a similar operation opened up the two

diagonal vistas. Apart from placing two small
obelisks in Upper Park (one of which is still extant),
no important alterations were made in the garden
during the next 40 years. So this was the old-
fashioned garden surveyed by Woodward in the
1770s.

Ten years after his plan was made, there were
great changes. The formal garden was swept away,
and before long the house was surrounded by the
grass and maturing trees of a landscaped park, as
Neale portrayed it in 1823. The old park, with the
enclosed fields surrounding it, had been of some 210
acres (including the Decoy Pond Field across the
main road). The present shape and extent of the
park, 399 acres, is due to Henry Bankes the Younger,
who, within two years of the Enclosure Act of 1784,
began enlarging and landscaping the park in all
directions, especially when the line of the Blandford
turnpike road was moved further out to the north.
Only the keeper's cottage remains from the small
hamlet of Kingston. Lists of trees dated 1789–90
include '24 Beech, 12 Spanish Chestnut, 6 Planes

of sorts' and 2,000 two-year-old beech for the woodland belts which he planted on the new park boundaries. The lists also comprise vegetables, fruit trees, ornamental shrubs and quantities of Portugal and common laurel for evergreen ground cover, which still thrive on the south side of the garden. By 1811 he had extended the park eastwards to Hill-butts, when it assumed its present shape, and the Blandford and Wimborne drives were established.

The present aspect of the park, dotted rather than clumped with mature trees, reflects successive plant-ing in the nineteenth century. William Bankes, like his father, was immediately active on coming into the property, planting in 1835 both the cedar avenue and the great two-and-a-half-mile beech avenue leading past Badbury Rings, according to George Evamy, a retired gardener speaking to Albert Bankes late in the last century. The bills for these have not yet been found, but some of the existing trees in both avenues can be dated to the 1830s. William wrote to his brother George in December 1837 of dining in London punctually at

half past six with the Duke of Wellington, who, ten years earlier in 1827, had visited Kingston Hall to lay the foundations of the Egyptian obelisk and to plant two or three cedars, and then catching the Exeter Mail at Apsley House at half past eight and 'choosing the Blandford post that I might see my whole avenue'. In 1838 quantities of young trees were being raised in a nursery on the estate, including oak, ash, scotch fir, hazel and thorns.

Henry Bankes wrote of his 'spacious lawn' and his son William began to re-formalise the garden with Barry's terrace on the south side and his garden sculpture shown in Philip Brannon's engraving, published in the third edition of Hutchins's *Dorset* (1868). In September 1853 William wrote from Paris with instructions to plant only violets in the border below the terrace, as anything higher would disturb the architecture, and that 'the great marble tubs' (the six well-heads) were to be permanently planted with bay trees. These bays are not shown in the engraving but appear in the photographs of 1900 and have now been reinstated. His letter goes

One of the Rosso Veronese lions on the south lawn

on to specify deal box covers to protect the sculpture in winter, and Kingston Lacy is one of the few places where this practice, now being followed everywhere in the Trust's gardens, has continued uninterrupted, though the boxes were painted white and not green as he wished. Evamy, the old gardener, described a wood cover for the obelisk, 'but it was let run to decay'. The focal point is the Philae obelisk, finally erected in 1839, but the Italian well-heads were set up only in the early 1850s. There is a seductive drawing by Barry for an elaborate formal 'terrace flower garden', entered from the loggia steps on the east, but this scheme was not carried out.

SCULPTURE ON THE TERRACE AND SOUTH LAWN

1 Four Verona marble 'upright vases' by Bartolomeo Barrini, 1847, each supported by four bronze tortoises by Carlo Marochetti, 1853. 'Think of my carrying a live Tortoise in a bag all the way from the Palais Royal!', wrote William from Paris to his sister in October 1853, 'when you see it multiplied to the number of sixteen'.

2 A 'pair of bronze vases with cupid handles from Versailles', purchased for 68 guineas at Christie's in 1841. Several Paris bronze founders copied thirteen original designs at Versailles, this pair predating the 46 ordered by Lord Hertford for Bagatelle near Paris in 1854, some of which are now at Sissinghurst in Kent, Lanhydrock in Cornwall, and the Wallace Collection in London.

3 Ten bronze 'vases' from Marochetti's workshop. The sockets on the balustrade were for poles to support a striped awning slung from the bronze rings above on the façade.

4 A pair of *Rosso Veronese* lions commissioned from Giuseppe Petrelli of Padua, January 1848, smaller versions of those at the foot of the Capitol in Rome.

5 Eight Carrara *tazze* ordered from Micali of Leghorn for 600 lire, November 1852.

6 A pair of bronze 'Versailles' urns copied from No. 2 above in 1992–3.

7 *Tazze* similar to No. 5 above and the marble seat

at the end of the gravel path added by Mrs Bankes, 1911, and a pair of bronze vases beyond the Dutch garden, 1912.

8 A pair of nineteenth-century bronze lions cast by Comperot.

WELL-HEADS ON THE SOUTH LAWN

The six well-heads or 'marble tubs' for bay trees are the work of William and his carvers in Verona from 1847 to 1851. One of the red marble examples was 'copied at Verona full size from one in the court of a palace of the Bevilacqua family' by the Montresor workshop. Another 'on which I have endeavoured to represent by boys the four seasons ... is my most considerable design in figures' and was carved in Istrian marble by Angelo Giordani. Two are old ones from the courtyards of 'Palazzo la Bernardo' and 'Palazzo Breganza' in Venice.

OBELISK

William Bankes first saw his pink granite obelisk in 1815. It is the eastern of a pair raised in front of the temple of Isis on the island of Philae, now inundated. It bears the names of Ptolemy VII Euergetes II, who died in 116BC, and his second consort Cleopatra III and records the exemption granted to the priests of Isis from bearing the expenses of the local administration, which, according to their petition, were ruining the temple. It arrived in England in 1821, when the Duke of Wellington offered to send it down to Dorset on a gun carriage. He came to Kingston Lacy to lay the foundation stone in April 1827. Linant de Bellefonds sent the remaining fragment of the companion obelisk and the three huge steps of granite from Maharraga to form the platform in 1829, but it was not finally erected until 1839. It had been damaged in transit on its long journey and was repaired with granite from the ruins of Leptis Magna given by George IV.

SARCOPHAGUS

It was made from Aswan granite for Amenemope, chief steward of Amun in Thebes during the early reigns of the nineteenth dynasty (1307–1250BC). He ended his career probably while Rameses II was king of Egypt and his tomb is in the Theban necropolis at Luxor. Henry Salt, the British consul, gave it to William Bankes and wrote in January 1822 hoping it would 'form an acceptable addition to your Egyptian antiquities'.

LATER HISTORY

William's brother George was responsible, according to Evamy, for 'a short avenue of Elms on the North side of the Park going to the Tradesman's Entrance', shown on the 1885 Ordnance Survey plan (to the south-east of the new entrance made by the Trust 100 years later) and removed in 1976 because they had succumbed to Dutch Elm disease. Walter Ralph Bankes extended the lime walk in the 1870s, laid out Nursery Wood outside the park to the south, and the kitchen garden, and was active in the park, also planting another cedar drive towards Wimborne and erecting an obelisk to mark Queen Victoria's Golden Jubilee in 1887. The date of the fernery is not yet known, but it must have been made for him in the late nineteenth century. A collection of period hardy ferns, and in particular forms of the Male fern, is now being established. Walter Bankes kept a brown owl in the brick house

Red Devon cattle were introduced to the park by Walter Bankes in the late nineteenth century

by the fernery and introduced the celebrated herd of Red Devon cattle.

On the east side of the house is the 'Dutch garden', laid out with golden yews clipped as 'skittles and balls' in 1899 by C.E. Ponting, the Salisbury diocesan architect who designed the church at Pamphill (see Chapter Ten). These beds are planted exactly as they were in Henrietta Bankes's time with pink begonias and blue heliotrope edged with pansies or wallflowers for spring flowering and snow-in-summer for summer colour. William Goldring of Kew was consulted for planting schemes from 1899 to 1906, most of which do not appear from photographs to have been carried out, except for the sunken garden, now restored to the original conception of fibrous-rooted begonias and hardy fuchsias. Mrs Bankes was also fond of red pelargoniums, and the cultivar 'Paul Crampel' has been replanted in the terrace borders. The origin of the Blind Walk is not clear and in particular the colour scheme of red and yellow, but with the help of Mr Edward Dukes, the retired head gardener, much new planting has taken place.

The Cedar Walk is lined with one of the Duke of Wellington's cedars, planted in 1827, and commemorative trees planted from 1905 to 1935 by visiting royalty and members of the family. A range of large-cupped narcissus cultivars is being developed in front of the nearby shrub border. The path turns left at the sundial down the ancient Lime Avenue to Nursery Wood, with a collection of specimen trees, and Spoon Walk, planted with rhododendrons and azaleas for spring effect, whence the visitor can return to the house via the Cedar Avenue. Wild flowers are a feature of the wood and careful grass-cutting is encouraging their range to increase.

On 25 January 1990, and in subsequent gales, Kingston Lacy suffered grievously, many important trees near the house and in the garden and park being blown over, including mature cedars, oaks and planes. Much of the shelterbelt of beeches was destroyed and 30 beeches in William Bankes's beech avenue. Clearing and replanting began immediately, accelerating the Trust's park planting programme. The beech avenue has been doubled by planting outer lines of beeches.

CHAPTER TEN

THE ESTATE

Ralph Bankes's estate was one of the largest ever bequeathed to the National Trust. For more than three centuries his ancestors had been among the top ten landowners in Dorset, and at his death in 1981 his estate comprised more than 16,000 acres, including Studland and the coastal hills of Purbeck surrounding the ruins of Corfe Castle, Holt Heath and the Kingston Lacy Estate, north of the River Stour near Wimborne.

Although members of the Bankes family represented Corfe Castle in Parliament until the nineteenth century, since 1663 Kingston Lacy has been the family seat. Their imprint on this part of the estate is apparent in the mansion, park and the magnificent avenue of beech trees lining the Blandford road, as well as in the surrounding fields, farms and cottages. But, while the Kingston Lacy Estate is the living legacy of this influential family, it is also an historic rural landscape dotted with earthworks and buildings indicating nearly 5,000 years of continuous human occupation.

Since the bequest, archaeologists have uncovered primitive tools of Neolithic occupants and have found evidence of at least 100 Bronze Age barrows, Roman roads and settlements and ancient lines of Anglo-Saxon hedgerows and field formations. The history of the land also survives in the place names passed down through the generations. For instance, sheep grazing today in the village of Shapwick continues a tradition recorded almost 1,000 years ago, when the place was referred to as 'Scapwuik', an Anglo-Saxon word for sheep farm.

Because of the estate's royal associations, perhaps since Romano-British times, numerous references to it survive in medieval documents. Census records compiled prior to the Black Death of 1348 indicate that the manor at Kingston Lacy exceeded the already substantial village of Wimborne in both wealth and population. By the time the Bankes family purchased the estate in 1632–6, it was largely divided into fields, pastures and forests, and supported numerous farmers and cottagers in the villages of Kingston, Cowgrove and Pamphill. In an effort to organise estate accounts and determine the various types of lease held by his tenants, Henry Bankes the Elder commissioned William Woodward to survey the land in 1773. Many of the buildings included in the survey remain on the estate today, as do descendants of some of the tenants. The following paragraphs describe some of these historic places and later additions to the Kingston Lacy Estate, principally by W. R. Bankes in the late nineteenth century and his widow, Henrietta, between 1904 and 1923.

BADBURY RINGS

Less than a mile north-west of Kingston Lacy stands an Iron Age hill-fort that has dominated the landscape for more then 2,000 years. The three concentric rings of earth at Badbury Rings are the remains of ditches and ramparts of a fort built between the sixth and first centuries BC. One of 40 or so similar forts in the region, Badbury Rings was probably built by a tribe known as the Durotriges on a site that had been populated for centuries. Earlier Bronze Age inhabitants built the three mounded barrows south-west of the rings, and flints and stone tools unearthed in recent excavations attest to Neolithic settlements in the vicinity.

After the Romans subdued the Durotriges in AD43, they built roads that intersect in a copse north-east of the hill-fort. Badbury became significant as a crossroads, and excavations confirm that Romans occupied the area until at least the early fifth century AD. Referring to a place called Baddanbyrig, the *Anglo-Saxon Chronicle* perhaps gives the earliest form of the fort's present name, but local

The oak avenue, with St Stephen's church beyond

legends assert that the name is derived from *Mons Badonicus*, or Mount Badon, the site of King Arthur's final victory against the Anglo-Saxons around AD 500.

Although Badbury remained relatively rural in medieval times, the local administrative unit, comprising 100 hides of approximately 120 acres each, was named the Badbury Hundred after the hill-fort and the court and council would have met here twice a year for the hundred moot. The land itself was used for grazing and as a hunting chase after the de Lacy family, who held the estate in the thirteenth and fourteenth centuries, claimed its hunting rights.

While Brave Dame Mary defended Corfe Castle, Badbury Rings also saw action in the Civil War. A group of Clubmen, crudely armed countrymen in the South-West fighting neither for the King nor Parliament but only for the protection of their own property, made a stand at the fort against Parliament's New Model Army. The rings con-

89

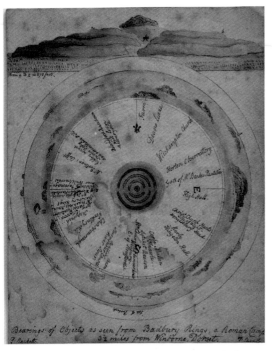

An eighteenth-century watercolour of 'Bearings of Objects as seen from Badbury Rings'. The National Trust has placed a bronze replica at the centre of the hill fort and has replanted the Scotch pines there to define once again the major vistas from the summit

special permission to hunt them in adjacent chases. Smaller animals, such as foxes, rabbits, hares, wildcats and fowl, were hunted in carefully managed warrens recorded here in the thirteenth century, and deer for the table were confined by ditches and fences in manorial deer-parks. In 1348 Alisia, Countess of Lincoln, complained that 'William of Tenge ... and others broke her park at Kyngeston Lacy and entered her free chase and warren there, hunted in these, cut down her trees there and carried away those trees and deer from the park and chases as well as hares, rabbits, partridges and pheasants.' The park keeper who probably lived here would have been responsible for preventing such a trespass, maintaining the ditches and fences, enclosing the hunting land and even feeding the animals in the winter.

Erected over a backfilled ditch surrounding an earlier deer-park, Lodge Farm has settled unevenly. Archaeological excavations undertaken during underpinning procedures in 1986–9 unearthed antlers and bones of polecat, rabbit, hare and peacock and confirmed that the present building replaced an earlier lodge, probably demolished in the late fourteenth century. The first floor contains a large hall, a defensive feature common in eleventh to thirteenth-century structures, but rare by the fourteenth century. The original trusses supporting the roof remain, as well as most of the original oak screen separating the common space from the adjacent private solar. Since 1740, when Badbury Warren was enclosed and converted into farmland, the lodge has been occupied by Kingston Lacy keepers and carters.

tinued to serve as a landmark on the Bankes estate. In 1761 the family planted pine trees to delineate the excellent vistas from its summit. Early in this century, Viola Bankes followed in the footsteps of her ancestors, riding here on horseback to feel 'mysteriously in touch with the primitive past'.

LODGE FARM

Lodge Farm, located between Kingston Lacy House and Badbury Rings, is known by legend as the hunting lodge of John of Gaunt, lord of Kingston Manor in the late fourteenth century, but was more likely built for the manor's forester and park keeper. Nevertheless, this first-floor hall house attests to the significance of hunting as a pastime for lords of the estate from Norman times. Only the King was permitted to hunt deer and wild boar in the royal forests, while clergy and nobility could be given

PAMPHILL GREEN AND
THE MEDIEVAL MOOT

In the thirteenth century the lords of Kingston Lacy were granted the right to run markets and began holding fairs on the common land at Pamphill Green. Still a gathering place today, this green contains evidence of some of the charitable contributions of the estate's wealthier residents. In 1698 Roger Gillingham, a merchant and native of Cowgrove, left money in his will to build an almshouse at the south-east end of the green. Although the building now serves as Pamphill First School, the eight doors in the wings flanking the central core still attest to Gillingham's provision of homes for four men and four women and a school with accommodation for the teacher in a loft above. The Bankes family contributed regularly to the upkeep of the almshouse and school. The group of small thatched cottages on the green east of the school, opposite the Vine Inn, was probably built during the late eighteenth century to ease the housing shortage caused by a growing population. According to the gardener George Evamy, the oak avenue was planted in 1842, during the exile of William Bankes. Henrietta Bankes initiated the Kingston Lacy Cricket Club in 1909 and built the cricket shelter and field that are still in use today.

Holly Lane, an ancient route preserved by the Trust as a footpath, leads from the south-west side of Pamphill Green to a more formal public gathering place, the moot court. Such a court is believed to have existed in the village of Cowgrove since Anglo-Saxon times and, although this curious open space surrounded by earth banks was once thought to be the foundations for the original manor house, it is now regarded as the place where the manor court heard matters of trespass, boundary disputes and changes in tenancy.

PAMPHILL MANOR

When Sir John Bankes purchased the estate at Kingston Lacy in 1632–6, it passed forever from royal ownership. Yet, despite the destruction of Corfe Castle and the building of Kingston Hall from 1663, for the tenants of the estate life probably remained much the same. Matthew Beethell became steward of the estate and oversaw its cottages and farms. In accordance with his important position, he occupied Pamphill Manor, perhaps the most substantial building on the estate, after the Bankes's new home. Beethell made extensive additions, encasing the old house within the new. At least five more substantial additions were made over the next three centuries. Evidence of the original core, in the form of Jacobean plank-and-muntin panelling and moulded heathstone plinths, came to

Pamphill Manor, the home of the steward to the Kingston Lacy estate in the late seventeenth century

light when the current leaseholder began extensive restoration. The ornate east front, with carved keystones, urn finials and central 'Dutch' gable, is part of an eighteenth-century enlargement.

FORGE COTTAGE

Until this century, skilled craftsmen had workshops in the area around Pamphill Green. Numerous carpenters, a wheelwright, a blacksmith and others had consistent work maintaining the mansion and gardens, as well as the cottages and farms of the estate. Although this cottage and adjacent forge probably date from the nineteenth century, the Woodward Survey indicates a blacksmith's shop at this site. The current buildings, probably built to replace the older house and forge, were used for more than a century by the Budden family, who shoed the horses for the estate and made and repaired iron objects used in the house, garden and farms. Frank Budden remained at the forge until the 1950s and many of his smithing tools remain here intact.

WHITE MILL

At the time of the Domesday Book, the manor at Wimborne produced enough grain to support eight mills along the Stour. By the fourteenth century, three of these mills, driven by the river's steady flow, were being used for scouring and cleaning cloth produced by the small wool industry in the

White Mill

area. White Mill, which produced flour, was built at Henry Bankes the Elder's initiative on a site occupied by mills for centuries. Although he died four years after inheriting the neglected estate in 1772, Henry oversaw massive improvements to the land, guided largely by the 1774–5 Woodward Survey he commissioned in 1773. Seeing that John Joyce, tenant of the Mill House, was not paying rent on the dilapidated mill, Henry replaced it with a double wheel straddle mill, recovering his approximately £300 expenditure by increasing Joyce's rent. A keystone over the mill's archway bears the date of the 1776 reconstruction but the masonry wheel pits of the older structure remain below. The Joyce family operated the mill until 1885, when Thomas Joyce switched from milling to farming and baking.

The sixteenth-century bridge, adjacent to the mill, crosses the Stour along an ancient route between Wimborne and Dorchester. A bridge was documented at this site in 1177 and in 1341 a man named Richard Bryan bequeathed money to repair the 'bridge at Wytemull'.

COWGROVE AND
BISHOP'S COURT FARMS

While the high ground around Badbury Rings was ideal for hunting and grazing, generations of farmers worked the arable land of the Stour Valley. Cowgrove and Bishop's Court are examples of numerous farms on the estate that continue this tradition today. Although the Domesday Book listed no cows on the estate, they were surely here by 1288 when Cowgrove was first recorded as 'Cougraue', meaning grove for cows. The farmhouse at Cowgrove dates from the nineteenth century, but was built on an older core, just as many of the farm buildings replaced older structures to adapt to modern farming practices. The Chissell family, in their fourth generation at the farm, cultivate fields that have been used by farmers for perhaps 500 years. One of the estate's older farm structures is an eighteenth-century granary at Firs Farm, on Cowgrove Road. The timber structure is raised on mushroom-shaped staddle stones designed to prevent rats from getting into the stored grain.

Bishop's Court Farm, at the western limits of the estate in the village of Shapwick, also has an elegant farmhouse, consisting of a large Victorian wing attached to an older core. The earlier section, constructed of heathstone, limestone and flint, has been identified as the remains of the manor house of Shapwick Champayne, the 'ancient seat of the Husey's ... long since turned into a farmhouse', according to Hutchins. The farm and house came into the Bankes family in the eighteenth century and the Woodward Survey records that its 465 acres included cow pastures, meadow and arable land. The Bankes family coat of arms and fleur-de-lis are visible on the north front.

ST STEPHEN'S CHURCH

The medieval manor of the de Lacy family included a family chapel dedicated to St Stephen. The chapel was presumably destroyed with the rest of the manor house in the fifteenth century and, until 1907, the Bankes family attended church at Wimborne Minster or Studland. When Walter Ralph Bankes died in 1904, he left £5,000 in his will for the construction of a chapel on the estate. His widow, Henrietta, carried out this wish and also made a variety of other estate improvements between 1904 and 1923 during the minority of her son, Ralph Bankes, whose initials they bear. Henrietta worked closely with the architect C. E. Ponting on a number of buildings, including additions to the family's summer house at Studland and this church. Although estate tenants attended St Stephen's, it was intended as a family chapel. Constructed of Portland stone and red sandstone quarried from the estate at Studland, the trusses in the nave were fashioned from oak grown in the park here. Above the family's elevated pew at the rear of the church are stained-glass armorial windows, previously in Wimborne Minster, representing three centuries of Bankes family marriages. Horace Wilkinson designed the new stained-glass windows at the front of the church which feature likenesses of the Bankes children, Ralph, Viola and Daphne. Appropriate to its name, the church also includes a statue of St Stephen, who stands above the main entry to the church with his hand on the head of the young squire, Ralph Bankes.

BIBLIOGRAPHY

The Bankes family and estate archive has been deposited in the Dorset County Record Office in Dorchester.

THE HOUSE

CAROE, M. B., 'Kingston Lacy, Dorset: an Architectural Case History', *ASCHB Transactions*, x, 1984.

CLEMINSON, Antony, The transition from Kingston Hall to Kingston Lacy', *Architectural History*, xxxi, 1988, pp.120–135.

CORNFORTH, John, 'Kingston Lacy revisited', *Country Life*, 17, 24 April and 5, 12 June 1986, pp.1016–19, 1123–7, 1576–80, 1674–7.

Country Life, 21 April, 12 May 1900; xv, 16 April 1904, p.558.

Gardens Old and New, i, Country Life, 1900, pp.265–70.

GUNTHER, R. T., *The Architecture of Sir Roger Pratt*, Oxford University Press, 1928, pp.98–116.

HILL, Oliver, and John Cornforth, *English Country Houses: Caroline*, Country Life, 1966, pp.26–31, 234.

HUTCHINS, Rev. John, *The History and Antiquities of the County of Dorset*, 1774; 3rd ed., iii, 1868.

JACKSON-STOPS, Gervase, *An English Arcadia 1660–1990*, National Trust, 1991, pp.134–7.

The Ladies' Field, 2 June 1900.

LATHAM, Charles, *In English Homes*, Country Life, 1904, pp.341–6.

MITCHELL, Anthony, *Kingston Lacy*, National Trust guidebook, 1987.

OSWALD, Arthur, *Country Houses of Dorset*, Country Life, 1935, pp.76–9.

RCHM, *County of Dorset, v, East Dorset*, HMSO, 1975.

SILCOX-CROWE, Nigel, 'Sir Roger Pratt 1620–1685', *The Architectural Outsiders*, Waterstone, 1985, pp.1–20.

THE ESTATE

The National Trust has made vernacular building surveys of Lodge Farm, Pamphill Manor, White Mill, and the farms and cottages.

BRIDGES, Sarah, and Martin Papworth, 'Kingston Lacy Manorial Buildings', *Dorset Archaeology*, 1991, pp.119–22.

CANTOR, L. M, and J. D. Wilson, 'The Medieval Deer Parks of Dorset', *Dorset Proceedings*, 1969.

LODDER, A. T. ed., *A History of the Principal Events during the Minority of Henry John Ralph Bankes*, Cox and Sharland Ltd, Southampton, 1904–23.

FAMILY HISTORY

BANKES, George, *The Story of Corfe Castle*, 1853; *Brave Dame Mary*, 1873 and 1924.

BANKES, Viola, *A Dorset Heritage: the Story of Kingston Lacy*, Richards Press, 1953; 2nd ed., Anthony Mott Ltd, 1986.

BANKES, Viola, and Pamela Watkin, *A Kingston Lacy Childhood*, Dovecote Press, 1986.

CLEMINSON, Antony, 'Christmas at Kingston Lacy: Frances Bankes's Ball of 1791', *Apollo*, December 1991, pp.405–9.

ROWSE, A. L., 'Byron's friend Bankes: a Portrait', *Encounter*, March 1975.

EGYPT

BANKES, W. J. ed., *Narrative of the Life and Adventures of Giovanni Finati*, 1830.

ČERNÝ, Jaroslav, *Egyptian Stelae in the Bankes Collection*, 1958.

DAVIES, Nina M., *Egyptian Tomb Paintings*, 1958.

IVERSON, Eric, *Obelisks in Exile*, ii, 1972.

JAMES, T. G. H., 'Egyptian Antiquities at Kingston Lacy, Dorset', *K.M.T.*, iv/4, winter 1993–4.

JAMES, T. G. H., 'Egyptian Antiquities at Kingston Lacy, Dorset', *Apollo*, May 1994.

MACLARNON, Kathleen, 'W. J. Bankes in Egypt', *Apollo*, August 1986, pp.116ff.

PICTURES

GORE, J. St John, 'The Bankes Collection at Kingston Lacy', *Apollo*, May 1986.

HARRIS, Enriqueta, '"Las Meninas" at Kingston Lacy', *Burlington Magazine*, February 1990, pp.126–30.

LAING, Alastair, 'Sir Peter Lely and Sir Ralph Bankes', *Art and Patronage in the Caroline Courts*, Cambridge University Press, 1993, pp.107–31.

LAING, Alastair, *In Trust for the Nation*, National Trust, 1995.

LAING, Keith, and Michael Hirst, 'The Kingston Lacy Judgement of Solomon', *Burlington Magazine*, April 1986, pp.273–86; and letters by Cecil Gould, August 1986.

MACLARNON, Kathleen, 'William Bankes and his collection of Spanish paintings at Kingston Lacy', *Burlington Magazine*, February 1990, pp.114–25.

SCULPTURE

WARD-JACKSON, Philip, 'Expiatory Monuments by Carlo Marochetti in Dorset and the Isle of Wight', *Journal of the Warburg and Courtauld Institute*, liii, 1990.

WARD-JACKSON, Philip, 'Carlo Marochetti and the Glasgow Wellington Memorial', *Burlington Magazine*, December 1990.

INDEX